An
Mili
1970

American Militarism 1970

A dialogue on the distortion of
our national priorities and
the need to reassert control
over the defense establishment

EDITED BY ERWIN KNOLL

AND JUDITH NIES MCFADDEN

Epilogue by **J. WILLIAM FULBRIGHT**

NEW YORK / THE VIKING PRESS

Editors' Preface

An event of unusual significance took place in Washington early in the spring of 1969. Under the sponsorship of members of the Senate and the House of Representatives, a "Congressional Conference on the Military Budget and National Priorities" was convened on Capitol Hill, March 28 and 29. The participants included Democrats and Republicans, as well as some who have abandoned all trust in the conventional politics of the two-party system; distinguished scientists and scholars whose counsel has been sought by administrations of both parties; and former government officials who enjoyed the confidence of Presidents Eisenhower, Johnson, or Kennedy.

In two days of wide-ranging deliberations they discussed the proposed anti-ballistic missile system and other aspects of the arms race; strategies for ending the Vietnam war and forestalling American involvement in future Vietnams; and possible techniques for restoring a measure of Congressional oversight to the burgeoning budgets of the Pentagon. They also dealt with the larger issues of the militarization of American foreign policy and domestic life, the need for redefining the national purpose, the prospects for restructuring American society. From their varied points of view, they produced a provocative and informative dialogue which served as the basis for a report subsequently issued by the Congressional sponsors.

The conference was patterned on a similar symposium on the Vietnam war held in January 1966 under the sponsorship of many of the same members of Congress and with some of the same participants. That conference arrived at a remarkably prophetic assessment of the war and a strong appeal for de-escalation which was, tragically, ignored at the time. We believe that the 1969 conference will prove no less prophetic in identifying the issues that will dominate public concern in the United States in the years to come.

Like its predecessor, the 1969 conference was intended primarily as a vehicle for informing its Congressional sponsors. Except for a brief opening session and a concluding press conference, the discussions were closed to the press and the public. When it was later proposed, however, to publish an edited transcript of the proceedings, the sponsors and participants responded with prompt and enthusiastic cooperation.

This book consists of the report of the Congressional sponsors and excerpts from the conference deliberations. In addition, Professor Kenneth Boulding of the University of Colorado, who was unable to take part in the conference, provided the material that appears under his name in Chapter IV, and Senator J. William Fulbright, Chairman of the Senate Committee on Foreign Relations, contributed the Epilogue.

The ten Members of Congress who initiated the conference were: Senators George S. McGovern of South Dakota and Gaylord A. Nelson of Wisconsin; Representatives George E. Brown, Jr., of California, Phillip Burton of California, John Conyers, Jr., of Michigan, Don Edwards of California, Donald M. Fraser of Minnesota, Robert W. Kastenmeier of Wisconsin, Benjamin S. Rosenthal of New York, and William F. Ryan of New York. The Introduction to this book was prepared under their direction. Representatives Robert C. Eckhardt of Texas and Abner J. Mikva of Illinois also assisted in the preparation of this book.

Other Congressional sponsors who signed the conference

report were Senators Fulbright, Harold E. Hughes of Iowa, Walter F. Mondale of Minnesota, William B. Saxbe of Ohio, Joseph D. Tydings of Maryland, Harrison A. Williams, Jr., of New Jersey, and Stephen M. Young of Ohio, and Representatives Hugh L. Carey of New York, Shirley Chisholm of New York, William L. Clay of Missouri, Charles C. Diggs, Jr., of Michigan, Jacob H. Gilbert of New York, William J. Green of Pennsylvania, William D. Hathaway of Maine, Augustus Hawkins of California, Ken Hechler of West Virginia, Henry Helstoski of New Jersey, Edward I. Koch of New York, Robert L. Leggett of California, Allard K. Lowenstein of New York, Patsy T. Mink of Hawaii, William S. Moorhead of Pennsylvania, Robert Nix of Pennsylvania, Richard L. Ottinger of New York, Bertram L. Podell of New York, Thomas M. Rees of California, Henry S. Reuss of Wisconsin, Edward R. Roybal of California, James H. Scheuer of New York, Louis Stokes of Ohio, Robert O. Tiernan of Rhode Island, Lester L. Wolff of New York, and Frank J. Thompson, Jr., of New Jersey. The report reflects an over-all consensus of the signers' views, although each of them does not necessarily subscribe to every conclusion or recommendation.

The editors are grateful to *The Progressive* magazine, in which the Congressional initiators' Introduction and the conference transcript originally appeared in somewhat different form.

ERWIN KNOLL
JUDITH NIES MCFADDEN

Washington, July 1969

Contents

Introduction: What Kind of Country?

By Senators George S. McGovern and Gaylord A. Nelson, and Representatives George E. Brown, Jr., Phillip Burton, John Conyers, Jr., Robert C. Eckhardt, Don Edwards, Donald M. Fraser, Robert W. Kastenmeier, Abner J. Mikva, Benjamin S. Rosenthal, and William F. Ryan

What kind of country do we want the United States to be? To what ends should the national will and the nation's tremendous resources be mobilized? What priorities should govern our public life in this last third of the twentieth century?

These questions are the underlying theme of this book. They are urgent questions, requiring immediate and intense attention. Many Americans believe that we have somehow gone astray, that we have lost sight of the American purpose and dissipated the American dream.

Existing institutions are failing to respond to the realities of our times. Societal structures can be stable and satisfying to those who live under them only when widespread agreement exists as to their basic values and purposes. There is no such widespread agreement today. Witness the social turmoil in our cities, on our campuses, in our churches, even in our homes. The social values implicit in our governmental decisions are no longer in accord with the needs strongly felt by large segments of our society.

Throughout this book, there are repeated references to "obsolete definitions" and "archaic concepts," perhaps best illustrated in Senator Fulbright's Epilogue on the meaning of national security. In contrast to our technological and scientific achievements, our political thought and social structure have remained primitive in conception and stunted in development —largely incapable of dealing with the situations our technological civilization has produced. In many ways, the dinosaur analogy is apt: we have created an enormous technological body with a tiny social and political mind.

As men in public office, we bear a special responsibility for addressing ourselves to the problem of institutional failure and the challenge of constructive change. Few Americans realize, however, how limited is the power of any individual member of Congress when he attempts to affect national policy. Each of us, in his own way, has been forced outside the institutional limits of Congress so as to gain new perspectives on how to make change possible.

In order to determine what might be our most effective course of action in fostering a re-examination and reordering of national priorities, we convened a closed meeting of some of the most able minds in the country to explore the nature of American society and examine some of the fundamental questions that must be asked about our economic, political, and corporate institutions. At the root of our concern was an awareness of the increasingly prominent role that military considerations, military objectives, and military expenditures have come to play in the nation's life. We initiated these discussions in the conviction that Congressional control of military policy must be reasserted and that the level of Congressional analysis of these critical issues can be raised through a greater intimacy between the legislative branch and the intellectual community. Our purpose was to articulate the basic issues of the militarization of American society for the general public as well as for Congress, and to examine concrete proposals for restoring democratic control over the military budget. The substance of our discussions is included in this book, but two principal themes should be underscored.

The first is the nature of the national security bureaucracy itself. It is composed of the armed services, the Central Intelligence Agency, the National Security Agency, the Atomic Energy Commission, and other bodies provided for in the National Security Act of 1947. It is closely linked to the aerospace and armaments industry, segments of the labor movement, universities with defense research contracts, and a new class of scientists, engineers, and businessmen. This complex is not a conspiracy; it is an enormous, self-perpetuating institutional organism. It receives such a disproportionate amount of federal funds that there is no effective counterbalance to it, and decisions such as those made on the Vietnam war and the anti-ballistic missile are generated from institutional momentum rather than conscious policy. Yet the power to make such decisions is—and in a democracy must be—the function of a political system responsive to the people, not the self-asserted prerogative of a bureaucracy that answers solely to itself.

Second, to reassert control over this enormous bureaucracy we must take a new look at America's role in the world, reassess our own social, economic, and political institutions, and redetermine our national priorities. Congress cannot undertake this task alone. It must be guided by the broadest possible public debate, for without such debate we shall be unable to translate public anxieties into political understanding and thus forge a new political will to reverse present policies.

This debate must be taken up by local organizations, political clubs, university groups, and every individual man and woman who cares about the society he lives in. A fundamental decision must be made by all of us, and that is how we want our tax dollars to be spent. We are heavily taxed by federal, state, and local levies. Even with added sales taxes, gasoline taxes, surtaxes, not enough money is generated to provide for such necessary services as schools, public transportation, parks, pollution control. The pattern is nationwide.

The urgency of our concern is underscored by the critical juncture at which we stand in the development of nuclear weapons. The reason we call for the postponement of ABM deployment, a moratorium on testing of MIRV (multiple independently targetable re-entry vehicle), and immediate commencement of strategic arms talks with the Soviet Union is that the opportunity for an international arms limitations agreement may soon be severely diminished. Because of the impossibility of detecting the number of warheads inside a deployed missile, we shall soon reach a stage when neither superpower will want to accept a limitation on its strategic force.

Unless we act decisively, the opportunities for slowing down the arms race in the next decade may become almost nonexistent. The bureaucratic momentum of the defense establishment, with its parochial view of the world, is projecting decisions that are contrary to the needs of the nation and the well-being of mankind.

The staggering costs of this proposed arms spiral cannot be measured accurately in dollars or as a percentage of the gross national product. The proper measures are in opportunities foregone. Shall we fund a new strategic bomber—or provide Upward Bound summer courses for 600,000 ghetto students with college potential? Shall we permit excessive contractor costs to go unchecked—or provide Head Start education for two and a quarter million additional children plus enough school lunches to feed twenty million children for a whole year? Shall we spend this year's Safeguard funds—or train 510,000 more hard-core unemployed?

In the decade from 1959 to 1968, direct defense outlays of the United States came to more than 551 billion dollars. This is twice the amount spent for new private and public housing in the same decade, and nearly twice as much as federal, state, and local governments allocated to education. In 1969 alone a conservative estimate of military-related spending amounted to more than 106 billion dollars, constituting almost eighty per cent of appropriated federal funds. This was more than *all* federal, state, and local expenditures on heath, hospitals, education, old-age benefits, welfare, unemployment, and agriculture.

This order of priorities prevails at a time when twenty million Americans live in dilapidated, rat-infested housing while the building industry cannot even keep up with the population increase and is in fact declining in productivity; when there are at least ten million victims of malnutrition and untold thousands of children with permanent brain damage because of insufficient food; when close to forty million people live in poverty with little access to medical or welfare care; when millions of children are doomed to lives of misery and poverty because of inadequate or nonexistent school facilities.

The degree of economic damage done each year by the massive allocation of resources to military spending has been noted by such economists as Kenneth Boulding, who points out that the economy's growth rate has been diminished by as much as two per cent per annum as a result of the diversion of resources into "the rat hole of competitive weapons systems, or even space technology."

Unlike investments in education or new factories, expenditures for missiles add nothing to the nation's productive capacity, although they do generate income for a certain segment of the population. Other costs are just as great, although less easily quantified. Civilian businesses suffer because they cannot match the salaries offered by subsidized defense firms; scientists and engineers are trapped into doing research that is contrary to life-saving causes; a new class of business executives arises—of men who know little about marketing or cost controls but who know how to negotiate effectively with government officials.

The most striking evidence of the decay of our society is that we have sought to meet the local crises of race and poverty by increasing militarization—by training more than

400,000 National Guardsmen and police in local riot control. The pervasive use of military means to solve our social and political problems is the most alarming indication of the emptiness of other conflict-resolving institutions.

In many other subtle ways individual values and ideals have been eroded. We are slowly becoming conditioned to the acceptance of regimentation, wire-tapping, snooping, and spying by large national and internal-security agencies. In many communities the existence of defense installations has retarded necessary social reform by reinforcing prevailing patterns of racial segregation and economic rigidity. In industry the military have taken over fundamental business decisions, even necessitating security clearances for business executives. Some of the nation's best minds have been induced to devote their creative talents to military enterprises, while pressing social problems fester in neglect.

Eventually we must recognize that the factors which determine our massive military budget are to be found not so much abroad as at home. The reason we are able to move a wounded Marine from the jungles of Vietnam to the finest medical care in minutes, yet cannot do the same for a sick child on the Mississippi delta or on an Indian reservation, is very much bound up in our image of ourselves.

Being the greatest power in the world carries psychological implications which many of us have not yet truthfully faced. We do a great deal to buttress that image of power; other sacrifices we find harder to make. We are six per cent of the world's population using more than sixty per cent of its goods and developed resources. We are convinced that the American way of life is the best in the world, that American management and enterprise are the best in the world, and that capitalism is the best tool for development. Our foreign policy is not dictated as much by external threats as we would like to think, but is an extension of our own economic, political, and social institutions. If anti-Communism is all we can agree on as a national credo, we will never be able to break the psychosis of force and destruction which is the American tragedy.

Our national priorities were set out in the Constitution. Somehow we have forgotten them. The priorities of our forefathers were "to form a more perfect union, establish justice, ensure domestic tranquillity, and to provide for the common defense." Our first task is to reinterpret these great goals in light of the realities of the twentieth century and the dawn of the twenty-first century.

"To form a more perfect union" is to end the racism and discrimination that have long permeated American life. "Our society is moving toward two societies, one white, one black—separate and unequal." The extraordinary Kerner Commission Report on Civil Disorders outlines the deepening of the racial division in our country. To continue on our present course can only lead to the fragmentation of America into increasingly violent and repressive factions and to the ultimate destruction of basic democratic values. Talk as we will of strength and wealth and power, we are a weak and divided society.

To form a more perfect union is surely our first task.

"To establish justice" is to end the exploitation of the poor and the weak and to make our legal system one that insures we are governed by laws and not by men.

At a time when we have equated justice with law and order, it is important that we take a look at the "crime" in our society. The crime we talk about in America is crime in the streets. What about the crime of a society which would shoot a sixteen-year-old for looting a television set but think nothing of hungry children in a land of surplus food? What is not talked about is the crime of a society with dual standards of justice, where property is protected at any price while the costs of extortion, price-fixing, rake-offs, restraint of trade through duress or threat, blackmail, and consumer frauds are either ignored or passed on to the citizen in the form of higher prices. Organized crime drains the body politic of an estimated 22 billion dollars per year. This crime does not appear in the statistics, but it erodes the moral fabric of our society and gives a hypocritical ring to cries for law and order. The real issue is justice.

"To ensure domestic tranquillity" is to redefine the difficult yet essential role of the police in contemporary society; to assist them in becoming more effective and creative servants of a pluralistic society; and to make sure that their function is not reduced to that of being mere agents of a local power structure. The continued training of police and National Guardsmen in military techniques will not eliminate the economic and social failures which generate discord and disruption.

In the next five years twenty million Americans will leave the rural poverty in which they no longer can eke out a livelihood and migrate to cities which cannot house, feed, educate, or employ them. Massive disorder will be the probable result.

In the next few years many more students can be expected to rebel against institutions which allow them no real responsibility, offer them careers they find abhorrent, and send them off to die for wars in which they cannot believe. They will challenge the only segment of society over which they have any control: schools and universities.

The police and National Guard can quell riots, but they cannot bring tranquillity. "There is no more urgent task than to break down the walls of isolation which surround our local police," warned the President's Commission on Law Enforcement. The redefining and reorganization of our entire system of law enforcement—police, courts, and correctional apparatus—are essential to ensuring domestic stability and tranquillity.

"To provide for the common defense" means in the nuclear age to find new ways of leading in international cooperation, of building international institutions which can provide effective arms control and disarmament. The common defense does not require an American force for every conceivable contingency, however remote, nor does it require an endless arms race of nuclear and thermonuclear weapons which, if used, would destroy exactly what we are trying to protect.

A single nuclear exchange between the United States and the Soviet Union would claim at least 120 million American lives. To offer up a large percentage of our population as a human sacrifice is not to provide for the common defense.

The current strategic plans of our armed forces do not meet their Constitutional obligations as historically defined. To provide for defense in the nuclear age is to formulate and carry through a policy aimed at a stable peace. It means, at this point in time, a moratorium on further MIRV testing, no further ABM deployment, and successful arms limitation and disarmament agreements with the Soviet Union and other nations. A policy which is consciously directed toward creation of a stable peace and which allows for profound change in the third world must now be fashioned to provide for the common defense of the United States.

How can we readjust our national priorities to the realities of today? It is clear that President Nixon will be no more able to control military spending than were Presidents Johnson and Kennedy. The very size of our national security institutions precludes any partisan responsibility. The most urgent challenge confronting Congress today is to reassert control of the military bureaucracy and the policy decisions it has preempted.

This can be accomplished only by effective Congressional leadership backed by a broadly-based, informed, and concerned public constituency. In recent years the military budget and weapons policies have been determined by the Pentagon and by the Armed Services Committees of Congress without critical evaluation by the entire Congress or by the public. In 1968 the House Armed Services Committee held months of hearings on the military budget, but of hundreds of witnesses only two were not employees of the Pentagon.

The size and complexity of the military budget make effective review almost impossible once the appropriations measures reach the floor of either house. Some of our colleagues would like to impose a ceiling on the military budget of 50 billion dollars (which would be twenty per cent over the Soviet Union's military budget). An attempt should be made to analyze the budget on a line-item basis, which would permit us to explore the policies underlying the equipment we are asked to vote on. If we are asked, for example, to vote millions of dollars for high-speed troop transport, we should ask whether or not we *want* to be able to move troops around the world to various trouble spots at a moment's notice. And if we do, we must understand why. Our policies should determine our weapons and not vice versa.

This book reflects a new depth and awareness in the public mood which for the first time seems ready to translate concern into effective action. It is our hope that the book will serve as a catalyst to develop similar debates across the country which will allow us to assert our position as legislators for programs of the future rather than as speechmakers on the problems of the past.

I

The National Security Establishment

Our country is in danger of becoming a national security state. Since the end of World War II we have spent more than one trillion dollars, or two-thirds of the total expenditures of our federal government, on armaments and armed forces. Today, almost eighty per cent of our federal appropriations are allocated to defense and defense-related costs—an amount greater than all federal, state, and local outlays for Social Security, health, education, housing, and agriculture. And yet the military budget continues to increase each year, spurred by a seemingly self-propelled mechanism which operates with little or no attention to merit or national need.

In spite of these vast expenditures, and in spite of the security establishment which dominates much of our national life, Americans feel less secure than ever before. While external threats have receded in importance, many of our countrymen believe their nation has lost its way, and they feel a growing threat from within our cities. Many now ask whether the major threat to the security and well-being of this country arises from the possibility of attacks from without, or the possibility of decay and disintegration from within.

The constellation of federal institutions created by the National Security Act of 1947—the Department of Defense, the National Security Agency, the Central Intelligence Agency —as well as the Agency for International Development and the Atomic Energy Commission, have established and developed the bureaucratic base for an extensive national security apparatus. This apparatus is supported and buttressed by the new breed of federally subsidized corporations that produce hardware for the military. The labor unions too have been brought into this structure; more than three and a half million civilian workers are directly involved in national security programs.

Vast and varied armaments have been built—land armies, seaborne and airborne forces—all in the name of flexibility and greater freedom of action. We have failed to recognize that the ability to wield this force generates a powerful temptation to use it. The very existence of these forces places greater demands upon our civilian leadership for wisdom and restraint, qualities which, as we have sadly learned in Vietnam, are lacking in our political system today. And, through the system of security classification, this apparatus has been liberated from the normal restraints of public debate and Congressional judgment, even as its power grows and its ability to intervene in new conflicts increases.

The national security establishment was created in response to what we perceived, two decades ago, as an immediate threat to our nation's survival. Today we are learning that, much as we may differ in economic and philosophic terms with Communist countries, they are as interested in coexistence, and as concerned with economic development, as we. No other country has extended its military influence around the world in the way we have, and yet we continue to feel insecure—but now this insecurity reflects deep concern for the internal fabric of our own country. While we have been at our most powerful, in a strictly military sense, during the past few years, our prestige around the world and our influence with foreign governments have diminished markedly, as our position of leadership and our reputation for wisdom have suffered under the impact of a misguided intervention in Vietnam.

Among the goals of the Kennedy Administration which took office in 1961 was to establish greater civilian control over the military. Ironically, the undeniable result of unifying the operations of the armed services and introducing techniques of computer management was to increase the role of military considerations in determining American policy. Power once checked by rivalries and inefficiences is now wielded as a single force defying democratic control. From this perspective the debate over the ABM can be seen as a test of whether or not this power is cast in concrete for the next generation. If the ABM or the war in Vietnam cannot be stopped, the impotence of our political institutions will be manifest.

We now see that the institutions comprising the national security establishment reinforce each other and eliminate the effectiveness of countervailing institutions. Unless we view our continued military buildup as an institutional problem, we shall be unable to make any lasting change in the direction of our society or our foreign policy.

We should be clear on one point: The present situation has been created not by the uniformed military but by the nation's civilian leadership and the institutions it has developed to centralize and expand the national security functions. The military has been asked to make decisions and accept responsibilities for which it was not prepared, either by professional background or by the structure of military organizations. Too often responsibility was abdicated to the military for making broad policy choices, for defining the threats—and therefore the priorities—facing this country, and for determining the proper response to these threats. These assignments exceed by far the traditional tasks of developing battle plans and training men to carry them out.

It is customary for military leaders to plan on the basis of a "greater than expected threat." They assume that the Soviet Union will produce more intercontinental ballistic missiles than one might ordinarily expect, a larger anti-ballistic missile system, and so on. Having made these assumptions, it is not surprising that they propose enormous appropriations and gigantic procurement programs "to meet the threat." It is at the civilian policy-making level that there has been repeated failure. For it is the civilians who should look beyond these military projections to the effect of the proposed measures on our domestic society and on our foreign policy. *They* should arrive at a realistic total perspective, rather than expect it of the military.

The abdication of civilian responsibility and the loss of

balance in the exercise of national choices have produced a dangerously distorted situation. Today, the civilian policy-makers have become an intrinsic part of the military apparatus, attuned to its viewpoint more than to a wider national perspective. Just as the introduction of sophisticated weapons technology has "civilianized" the military, causing colonels to become the purveyors of abstract analyses and the silent partners of corporate managers, so the availability of these weapons in larger quantities has militarized the civilian hierarchy, leading it to seek answers to political problems in military hardware and enabling it to "project our power" over much of the globe.

The problem to which we must address ourselves is how to resist this interwoven bureaucracy, so large and entrenched, so zealous and parochial, so unrestrained by any effective counterbalancing force in our society. Conjuring marginal or imagined "threats" to justify its continued existence, it is itself a threat to our society, disturbing its tranquillity and jeopardizing the survival of freedom within it. Just as we have built up this apparatus over the past twenty-five years, we must now begin to reduce its size and influence.

Mr. Goodwin: What do we mean by the national security? It is against this question that all our defense efforts must be measured.

To the founding fathers, as to us, the national security was more than the survival of our citizens or the inviolability of territory. It was more than abundance and prosperity for the nation. It required us to maintain the kind of society we were meant to be—strengthening union, enlarging liberty, and extending justice to all who made this their home.

Should we win every battle, overwhelm every foe, and swell in strength until none dare tempt our might, and in the process be diverted from these pursuits, then we will have lost our national security. We may conceivably be more secure. But it will be our nation no longer.

Therefore, those of you who struggle to feed the hungry

and bring justice to the black man, who oppose any who would burden us with unnecessary armaments at the expense of human wants, who resist the effort to shape our national destiny with the weapons of fear for the many and secret information for the few—you are as much defenders of our national security as the industrialist who makes our missiles or the general who commands them.

For thousands of years the most primitive requirement of national security was the ability to defend against destruction. Then, in 1945, at Los Alamos, in a single flash, that possibility dissolved forever.

In 552 B.C., King Croesus of Lydia asked the Delphic Oracle, "Shall Croesus send an army against the Persians?" The reply came that if he should send an army against the Persians he would destroy a great empire. Croesus attacked, and his own empire fell. Our own oracles, the computers of the Pentagon, yield the same message. But this time there is no ambiguity.

We can destroy an adversary, but we are defenseless. Thus, safety now depends on preventing conflict and not on winning it. It is a painful thing to live in so hazardous a time. Yet if danger spurs us to look beyond our missiles and alliances to more fundamental demands of national security, then perhaps peace will be born of peril just as war has so often been the child of complacency.

It does not denigrate our very real achievements—from the Marshall Plan to the test ban and nonproliferation treaties—to say that we are today no closer to establishing the conditions of lasting peace than we were when our great global adventure began. The reasons for this failure are many, and much is in the hands of the global realists: those who proudly proclaim their tough-minded pragmatism. Theirs is a policy that leap-frogs the continents seeking, as best it can, to put down hostile forces wherever they emerge and supporting the *status quo*— any *status quo*—that does not appear to be our enemy.

This is the policy that supported Batista and ended up with

Castro, encouraged the Latin American military and lost an oil company, led Marines into the Dominican Republic and exiles into Cuba. It is a policy that has failed to maintain a common purpose among the Atlantic nations, forfeited our influence with the Arab states, helped to trivialize the United Nations. It is a policy that has failed to bring about the control of nuclear arms, which is clearly in the interests of both great powers—and led us to our first major military failure since the War of 1812.

In the grip of this policy, we still fight a war in Vietnam which, however it ends, will hardly have increased the confidence of others in our wisdom and strength. The Middle East is on the edge of conflict. A hostile China is becoming a nuclear power. The arms race is gaining momentum. And perhaps most seriously, in the eyes of much of the world—and especially among the young—we seem to have forfeited any moral right to leadership of the forces of liberty, justice, and wise restraint.

In fact, realistic policy has become virtually no policy at all, aside from maintaining the territorial *status quo* with Russia and China and hoping that Israel will survive. This policy has reached so sterile an ending because it is not guided by any clear perception of long-range goals or of the social and political forces at work on other continents. It lacks any ruling concept of the kind of world community in which we will be safest and most comfortable. It is, in other words, the ultimate romanticism of the ostrich.

Behind this policy lie deeply resistant attitudes. They are not some secret malevolence or hidden imperialism. There is, rather, timidity and the lack of confidence which makes it easier to move from crisis to crisis than to act when events do not demand action, or to withstand the pressure of immediate fears in pursuit of a long-range goal. The timidity is often matched with ignorance—ignorance as to where our own interests lie and what is really important to us. Many of those who talk most confidently about national interest know neither this nation nor its needs.

Of greatest interest, there is the growing militarization of our policy: not simply rising armaments but the even more dangerous tendency to rely on force and the calculations of force in dealing with world events. Increasingly, military men share in policy discussions for which they have little qualification or experience. This is not so much their fault as that of the civilian officials who heed them, and who often are fatally attracted to the kind of analysis which can be reduced to rigorous logic and fed into a computer. Thus, military plans for the Bay of Pigs were approved, even though any hope of success depended on Cuban hostility to Castro, for which there was no evidence. A military officer assured our highest officials that the Dominican rebels would lay down their arms when the first Marine resplendent in battle dress appeared on their beach. Twenty thousand troops later they still resisted, for no one knew what these rebels were like and what their convictions were.

In Vietnam, men as logical as Robert S. McNamara and General Maxwell Taylor each year—for six years—added up the forces on both sides and told us what it would take to "win." Yet the crucial factors were always the intentions of Hanoi, the will of the Vietcong, the state of South Vietnamese politics, and the loyalties of the peasants. Not only were we deeply ignorant of these factors, but because they could never be reduced to charts and calculations, no serious effort was made to explore them. No expert on Vietnamese culture sat at the conference table. Intoxicated by charts and computers, the Pentagon and war games, we have been publicly relying on and calculating the incalculable.

Those of us who are Democrats cannot look at the anti-ballistic missile, or other defense issues, as a source of partisan vindication. It was not so many years ago that generals were resigning in protest at President Eisenhower's refusal to yield to their demands for more arms. When Secretary McNamara took office, it was with the avowed aim of establishing greater civilian control over the military. Yet the harsh fact of the matter is that when he left, the military had greater influence over American policy than at any time in our peacetime history.

In the name of efficiency we unified many of the operations of the armed services, encouraged greater intimacy between the military and industry, and instituted the deceptive techniques of modern computer management, realistic or hardheaded, to solve problems and invest money and use power unguided by ultimate aims and values. This is thoughtless folly, for it destroys what it seeks to protect and ignores the realities of human faith and passion and desire. It is a force ultimately more powerful than all the calculations of economists and generals.

In the war-game rules and around the conference table we developed our options in the name of flexibility—amphibious forces, airborne forces, helicopter forces, special forces—seemingly unaware that when you have the ability to do something you will become powerfully tempted to do it. You can ask a computer if you have the military capacity to accomplish an objective. It will answer either yes or no. It will never say, "Yes, but it is not a good idea." It will not do to blame the generals. Force is their *business*. It was rather the civilian leadership which created this machine and gave it the tools to justify and explain and provide both the logic of fear and that exotic language of strategic theory which is used to baffle common sense.

It is only civilian leadership in Congress, as well as in the executive branch and in the political processes of this country, which can hope to keep our armed forces in rational relation to our needs. For a profoundly political issue is involved. That is whether the Pentagon is to play a fundamental and perhaps mortal role in shaping our national policy—using secret information, building an independent constituency through a vast public-relations program—while liberated from the normal restraints of public debate and Congressional judgment.

I know that it is often hard for a politician to resist those who claim the virtues of toughness and courage and patriotism. But it is easy to be tough when toughness means coercing the weak and rewarding the strong, and when men of power and influence stand ready to applaud. It is far harder to hold to principle, supporting forces temporarily repressed, enduring the frustration of long and inconclusive struggles, standing firm for ideals even when they bring danger. But it is the true path of courage. It is the only path of wisdom. And it is the sure path of effective service to the United States of America. It is also, I believe, the path the American people are seeking.

For 1968, with all its sorrows and failures, was finally a voyage of rediscovery, a journey to the springs of American hope. We did not find it in Washington or among the commentators. Rather, it was there waiting for us in Nashua and Concord and Manchester, in Madison and Racine and Eau Claire, in Oregon and California—the people of this country; decent, sure of instinct, desirous of peace, grateful for honesty, willing to face obstacles and strive against them—the repository of our strength, the source of our faith, the fiber of our will and high expectations. They are our national security. And they are still there.

Senator Nelson: In the brief period of six years that I have been in the Senate, no military budget has been subjected by the Congress—or by the public either—to really critical evaluation. We have passed seventy-billion-dollar military budgets after ten minutes or an hour of discussion, and whenever some of us attempted to offer modest amendments, it was a foregone conclusion what the result would be. We defaulted—the Congress and the public—in all matters of judgment on the military budget, on the theory that the military knew best and that we were dealing with purely technical military matters and not political ones. This has been our great mistake.

In the past three years, however, there has been a dramatic change: the military has lost its status of infallibility. This has been the lesson of our experience in Vietnam. If we could turn the clock back to the spring of 1965 and if we had the benefit of hindsight, is there a soul in the United States who would now advocate converting our mission in Vietnam from one of providing technical aid and assistance into that of waging a land war?

We relied upon military judgment and fell victim to colossal miscalculation. Distinguished military men testified at the time that the infusion of 50,000 or 75,000 troops into Vietnam would bring Ho Chi Minh to the peace table. That indicates how lacking in understanding they were of the nature and character of the war. That is why I, as one of three in the U.S. Senate, voted against the original 700-million-dollar appropriation and all appropriations to escalate the war in Vietnam.

I think Congress—or a good percentage of Congress—now recognizes that we have defaulted in our responsibility. I think a good part of the public now recognizes this, and they are asking that Congress and all the rest of the country participate in evaluating what we are doing, why, where we are going, and what for.

Professor Galbraith: We are not concerned in these discussions, I would suggest, with making the Pentagon more efficient. Secretary McNamara made as good an effort on that as could be made. We are not, I think, concerned with making the Pentagon and its suppliers more honest, or with eliminating graft. These things can, indeed, be diversions from the basic problem, and can leave the basic problem unsolved. We shall have accomplished little if we get out of Vietnam and leave uncontrolled the influences that were responsible for this disaster, for the Bay of Pigs, and for the Dominican Republic.

I would suggest, too, that we can't have a crusade against military men as such. Indeed, our purpose is to restore the military profession to its historic and honored role. The armed services were meant to be the servants and not the makers of national policy. They were never intended to be either un-limited partners or commercial subsidiaries of General Dynamics.

The problem is essentially one of bureaucratic power, un-controlled bureaucratic power which, in the manner of all bureaucracies, including those which many of us have been associated with, governs in its own interest and in accordance with its own parochial view of the world.

It is the problem of a vast bureaucracy going considerably beyond the Pentagon, embracing the intimately associated industries where increasingly the line between what is public and what is private can't be distinguished; and to all its out-riders and intellectual allies in the Department of State and the intelligence agencies, not to mention some members of the Congressional Armed Services Committees.

The principal instrument of power of this bureaucracy is fear. It is fear that gave it this enormous power and autonomy in the 1950s and early 1960s. This fear caused us to consoli-date and delegate power—in effect to say, "Here, we will give you all the money you can use, all the authority you need, and you deal with the danger of the Soviet Union and the Com-munist world."

It is interesting proof of the role of fear that Secretary of Defense Laird, when he was talking to Congress about the ABM, when he was seeking approval of the so-called "Safe-guard" system, immediately resorted to the tactic of trying to scare the hell out of everybody. I think one can say of the Secretary of Defense that he is a man who fully learns his business.

Since this power was born in an age of fear, it will be curbed only as we resist fear; only as we resist the temptation to scurry for cover when anybody talks about Communism; only as we look upon the world, Communist and non-Communist, with a certain calm intelligence.

I think we should also bear in mind that this is a power which traces to a period in our history not distant in time but quite different in character. This delegation of our power of the late 1940s and through the 1950s was in a period when it was possible to believe Secretary of State Rusk's haunting dream of a Communist imperium, completely united and probing out at any soft point on its perimeter and without— and with no objective short of the ultimate destruction of its opposition.

We must remind ourselves how distant that world is from the world that we now see: a world of bickering Communist states coming to the edge of actual conflict on some obscure island in Asia, a world where the Soviets have to move troops into Czechoslovakia "to have comradely talks." The most pregnant fear in the world today is the fear some Communist states have of other Communist states. There has recently been no depth of alarm in the West comparable to that felt in Yugoslavia and Czechoslovakia about the intentions of the Soviet Union.

There was another aspect of the 1940s and 1950s that we must also bear in mind. This was a period when the memory of the Great Depression was strong in all of our minds. In some measure we were spending money because we did not have an easy alternative to sustain employment. Liberals, those of us who went through that period, never liked to say that that was the nature of the federal budget, but it is in some measure the truth. In 1964 we were forced to reduce taxes essentially because we could not find civilian objects of expenditure that were acceptable to Congress.

We have now moved in less than a decade into a drastically different society in which the balance that all societies must sustain between their public and private outlays has been deeply disturbed. This is a practical matter. We must have a balance between what kids see on television and the quality of the schools they attend. We must have a balance between the concentration of urban work forces and what we do to make our cities livable. We must have a balance between our living standard and the enormous amount of refuse in which that living standard is packaged and which has to be disposed of.

It is a pervasive thing. For nearly twenty years we have allowed the enormous military budget to pre-empt a large part of the public expenditures which maintain this balance. We have had expansive private consumption and tight public expenditure designed to balance off this growth.

There is much psychological speculation involving race, the nature of poverty, and the like, to explain the agony of our cities. I am forced to confess to the somewhat old-fashioned view that damn few of these problems would not be substantially solved by a considerable increase in the budget.

Twenty years ago we were alarmed about the vision of the Communist imperium, but today most of us are much more alarmed about the crisis of our cities. Therefore, the ultimate task which confronts us is to bring the sense of priority that we have of our national responsibility abreast of the anxiety we all manifest.

I see this in no radical terms. I see only one possibility of doing this: through the Congress. Congress is the instrument which must do this. I don't think it will require great political sacrifice, because I think the public has come to share this concern.

Mr. Raskin: We are a great empire. And we are imperialists. We like very much being top dog in the world. That carries with it not only a psychology but a politics and economics. That is a point which I think has to be looked at very hard. I throw this out as a challenge, to see whether or not people are prepared to accept that view.

We must be prepared to ask: Do we want to be an empire?

Do we intend to be top dog in the world? Are we prepared to intervene all over the world? And are we prepared to pay that price? The price is a high one. The great Swiss historian Burckhardt said, "A great nation has only one purpose, and that is to get more power. But what it gives up in the process is freedom."

What we are really talking about is not only such questions as how large the standing army should be, whether the uniformed armed forces are different from the militarized civilian, and so forth, but the question of how the United States was actually transformed into a different sort of civilization, into a *national security state*. Should we attempt to control this national security state, to mediate it? Or should we assume the task of undertaking to dismantle it?

I would suggest that these turn out to be the two basic alternatives to which members of Congress and members of the scholarly community must address themselves. Do they think they can ride the tiger, mediating here, setting some sort of budgetary limits there, or are they prepared to undertake the more difficult task of dismantling the national security state?

A bulwark of the national security state is the Keynesian idea that a dollar spent on anything, no matter what, is equal to a dollar spent on anything else. We need a basic revision of our definitions of economic growth or we are going to be spending even more billions on madness, thinking that we are growing economically when in fact we are producing a negative effect on the society.

A whole series of systems and habits of mind has developed with the national security state. One is the classification system —the notion that the public must be denied access to information that everybody needs to make obvious moral and political judgments.

Secondly, there is the elaborate system of spying on citizens. We not only spy on people at the edges of the empire; it has become a habit of mind within the country itself.

There is the removal of decisions from public bodies such as Congress—except in those cases where particular Representatives and Senators operate as virtual permanent undersecretaries, such as the Defense Appropriations Subcommittee chairmen. The rest of the Congress becomes a talk group which arrives at no decisions and effects no real changes in the actual direction of our society. If Congress is unable to stop the war in Vietnam or change the direction on ABM, my judgment is that public bodies in this country will be nothing more than ornamental talk groups. They will have no effect on the actual policies of the nation.

The national security state has developed its own pension classes—large groups of people directly dependent on expenditures voted by Congress for old wars or new wars. Further, a substantial part of the educated class now depends specifically on the national security structure. The universities operate in part as its instruments. The engineers find themselves in a situation where they have to keep their laboratories hot because they have no other place to go. You may recall that in 1962 the only real reason given for the resumption of nuclear testing by President Kennedy was the fear that the engineers could not work, that we wouldn't be able to keep the labs going. We have built up a technological force that doesn't have any place to go, that doesn't fit into the business or commercial side of the economy.

Beyond that, the national security state has created an incredible malaise. The rhetoric of who we think we are and how we describe ourselves has nothing to do with who we really are and how we actually operate. We put billions and billions of dollars into killing, while we talk as if we really just love life. Part of the reason young people are so alienated is this contradiction between the rhetoric of how we describe ourselves and what is actually going on.

We find ourselves in a continuous situation of intervention and engagement, so that the American empire, if it continues to go in the same direction, will find itself constantly at war. One result of that will be that more and more black people will be fighting those wars abroad and will come back to become guerrillas at home. We will have guerrilla groups forming in the cities to attempt "national liberation," in their terms, from the situation that exists for them here.

I am not trying to scare anybody, but to provide a reasonable political, scientific analysis of the probable direction this country will go in if we don't undertake to dismantle the national security state.

Perhaps one place to begin is with the National Security Act of 1947. See what it has brought to America. See the groups that have attained power as a result of it. See its structure and begin to see how in fact that Act can be radically changed. Revise it.

Professor Galbraith: I would carry this line of argument one step further. Let me suggest that Mr. Raskin has raised a very real question but also, happily, one which is by way of solving itself.

As far as Latin America is concerned, as far as Asia is concerned, as far as Africa is concerned, there was a superpower complex shared by ourselves and the Soviets in the years immediately following 1945. We persuaded our people—I was in some degree one of those persuaded—that the world stood at a decisive watershed. The question in India, in the Congo, in Southeast Asia and elsewhere, was whether they would become part of the Communist empire or would follow another kind of development.

There was an assumption, certainly on our part and I think equally on the part of the Soviets, that the superpowers had an enormous capacity to influence the direction of the development in these countries. There was also an assumption, largely unexamined, that the nature of this development was of great importance militarily, economically, and otherwise to the countries involved.

In the last twenty years we have found out that these things simply are not true. Arthur Larson and I were at a meeting three or four years ago in Leningrad when the question came up as to what the difference was between a Communist jungle and a capitalist jungle; there was pretty general agreement that it was awfully hard to tell the difference between the two on just walking through.

We have learned that many other factors control the development of these countries. We have learned that lesson above all in Vietnam, where absolutely unlimited commitment of manpower and money has had a marginal effect. Under these circumstances, what we are concerned with here is an accommodation to reality. The empire to which Marcus Raskin referred was in large measure a figment of our imagination. It was something we thought we had and didn't.

The Soviets have made the same discovery.

For a very large part of the world, therefore, the withdrawal of military aid and the withdrawal of bases, the cutting back on off-shore naval forces, is merely an accommodation to that fact.

I can see, for example, no reason why we should spend more than five minutes debating the importance of military aid to Latin America. There is no case for it whatever. It was based on a misconception held by John Foster Dulles that Latin American armies had something to do with maintaining local peace, which we know to be not the case—a concept of continental security which couldn't be more ridiculous.

Professor York: I start from the position that in the present world we need military technology. The problem is not how to get rid of it but rather how to control it—how to prevent the creation of a twentieth-century Frankenstein's monster that could, despite all good intentions to the contrary, destroy us.

First of all, I would suggest that when listening to defense officials and officers we must insist on asking how a particular proposal or weapons system fits into the total national security picture and what its influence will be on the arms race. Surely the matter of the arms race itself is one of the most important factors bearing on our national security. One must not allow such questions to be brushed aside as too complex or because they involve some mysterious secret, and one must not accept without further argument such simplistic answers as, "It is an intrinsically defensive system and therefore not threatening." We have seen a singularly simple case of this last matter in connection with the ABM. The pro-ABM people have quoted no less an authority than Premier Kosygin as saying that ABM is defensive, therefore not threatening—and therefore not an accelerating factor in the arms race.

I would say to both Premier Kosygin and the Americans who quote him that our present multiple warheads program— the program we call MIRV—and the penetration aids programs are a reply to the first hint of a Soviet ABM system, and that, as anyone who has looked at the problem knows, the multiple warheads are one of the most serious factors in the arms race.

Another problem that I think must be dealt with differently than it has been in the past is the problem of secrecy. It must be dealt with on two quite separate levels. First and foremost, Congress must deal with it on the basis of its right as the people's representative to know what the big picture is and what is going on. No doubt some secrets are necessary, but we have gone much too far in classification. However necessary it may be to keep a secret, there is a price for each one, and that price is a diminution in our freedom—not much each time, perhaps, but of considerable consequence over-all.

For example, the deployment of major Air Force contingents to privileged sanctuaries in Southeast Asian countries such as the Philippines and Thailand and wherever else ought to have been reported somehow to Congress before it happened, rather than having it become something which had to be discovered later because it was too secret to talk about at the time. It is not enough to say that it was reported to some subgroup of Congress. Such select groups are nearly always unrepresentative of Congress and the country; they are composed of persons who, through long association with the military-industrial establishment, have developed an approach which heavily emphasizes purely military or technological solutions to what are basically political problems.

The second aspect of the secrecy problem involves defense officials who hide behind the phrase, "I have a secret which national security prevents me from revealing." The secret details—and, I repeat, I am not denying the validity of keeping some matters secret—are seldom essential to an understanding of the larger issues. As an example, I recall the occasion when a number of us were testifying before Congress about the ABM and brought up the matter of the short response time—which means that decisions to fire nuclear weapons have to be made at relatively low levels, and that the critical decision-making passes from statesmen to technicians, from high to low levels, and from human beings to machines. The next day, in the *Baltimore Sun*, there was a rebuttal to George Kistiakowsky, one of the persons who made these points, to the effect that unfortunately Dr. Kistiakowsky hadn't been briefed on the United States' most recent ideas about the command and control system.

Certainly the details of the command and control system have to be kept secret—what frequencies might be used and where the sending and receiving ends of the systems are. But the issue we were raising simply doesn't depend on those details but rather on the fact that the warning time available is somewhere between three or four minutes and perhaps twenty minutes or so. The basic factors involved in establishing the length of this warning time are not secret; they depend on the physics of the situation, on how far one point is from another, on where the launch point is and on where the terminal point is, on whether the launch point is far away in Siberia or close by. Therefore, the generalization which many of us have made —that the authority in these life-and-death decisions is passing from statesmen and politicians to low-level authorities and from people to machines—is a correct analysis of the trend of recent events. It cannot in my judgment be hidden behind claims that "you just don't understand about our command and control system." Maybe it is true that the Pentagon's 1969 ideas about something that won't be built until 1975 or so do not require a statesman to be present in the decision-making loop, maybe the communications are simple and secure and short, but the steadily increasing complexity and steadily decreasing warning times involved *are* moving us in the directions we described. Congress ought to question defense officials much more closely than it has, not just about the details but about the generalities, not just in such rare situations as the anti-ballistic missile hearings but much more often. Congress ought to seek reasonably expert but uncommitted advice.

I do not regard the ABM decision as a final step toward disaster, but rather as just one more step in the wrong direction. However, the discussion of the ABM has provided a unique opportunity to bring before the American public and their representatives, all of their representatives, a series of important questions which otherwise might never have come up. These questions ought to come up in connection with other defense matters, although for reasons of complexity, for reasons of secrecy, and so forth, they don't normally arise in such a neat form.

The ABM brought before us the whole issue of needlessly escalating technology and its relation to the arms race. It brought up the whole question of Congressional control over what is going on. It brought up the whole matter of secrecy and its use, and more importantly its abuse. It brought up the whole matter of decision-making passing from high to low levels, from statesmen to technicians, from human beings to machines. The ABM issue has provided us with an opportunity to raise questions in areas that otherwise are difficult to talk about. We have an opportunity to ask whether we are in fact getting more security from this technology, how much this purported additional security will cost, and what its ultimate effects will be.

Professor Kistiakowsky: It has been traditional, and I don't think exclusively in the United States, for military planners to make tentative plans and proposals on the basis of what is known as "greater than expected threats." Expected threats are those predicted by intelligence experts, and these predictions seldom err on the optimistic side. However, for military planning it is assumed that the threats are greater. For instance, it may be assumed that the Soviet Union will be able to destroy our Minuteman forces with the SS-9, equipped with precision MIRVs, and by means of some presumably classified means to neutralize our Polaris submarines.

Having made assumptions about the "greater than expected threat," military planners understandably provide military responses to the threats. This is their responsibility. But where the *real* responsibility lies, and where it has failed occasionally, is at the civilian policy-making level. It is the policymakers who are supposed to look beyond the projections of the military to ask about the social and economic impact of proposed measures on domestic society. They must also ask what effect these measures will have abroad, and what the response of our adversaries will be. Finally, they have to think about commitments we have made which they feel must be fulfilled. And out of that they must construct a system of realistic contingencies, not "greater than expected" contingencies, and plan on that basis.

This process has failed from time to time, and from my many years of knocking around Washington I would say that whenever a new civilian team moves into the Pentagon the failure is perhaps even a little larger than when that same team becomes more experienced.

Since the last years of the Eisenhower Administration a

process has taken place which makes the task of the civilian policy-makers more difficult. In 1959 and 1960, when I was watching it from close in, the assessment of military proposals was partly done from outside the Defense Department. A new office of Defense Director of Research and Engineering had only just been established. (Herbert York was the first to hold the office.) Since then, however, the office of the Secretary of Defense has become large, and while technically competent, it has become institutionalized, from a military point of view. Now the proposals come from all the services together, backed up by the office of the Secretary of Defense. The other civilian policy-makers, in the executive branch and in Congress, have accordingly a tougher job in challenging these proposals.

Yet I would like to suggest that an independent analysis is not impossible. The problems are complex, but they are not beyond any ordinary human intellect, providing one spends enough time on them.

Part of the difficulty is that the people in executive positions in the government have so many responsibilities that they can allocate only limited time to reaching decisions on even complex problems. That is why I like, for instance, the suggestion that James Killian made when he testified before the subcommittee of the Senate Foreign Relations Committee: that there be set up an *ad hoc* group of uncommitted, well-informed citizens who would look at some of these problems on a full-time basis. This would be a very helpful tool for the formulation of policy.

I think the present situation requires something bolder than merely arguing whether the ABM should or should not be deployed. I personally believe its deployment is undesirable, but it is not the end. The ABM is more a symptom of the trend than the central issue. I hope, therefore, that however the ABM debate comes out, it will not mark the end of efforts by the civilian part of the government, including Congress, to insist that there be a much sharper separation between the military planners and their proposals on the one hand, and those individuals who really must decide on the needs of the United States in the great complex of our foreign policy.

Mr. Walinsky: The discussion so far has assumed that our foreign problems have posed certain challenges to us and that our responses, while perhaps disproportionate, have at least *been* responses to these foreign problems. But the shift from the Eisenhower defense budget to the Kennedy defense budget should teach us that the military budget can be entirely unrelated to challenges as they are seen and perceived—that the real factors which determine our defense budget are to be found less abroad than they are here at home.

Professor Galbraith, for one, has demonstrated the extent to which our prosperity and growth have been built on a corporate system which depends on the defense budget for almost all of its technological innovation and for a tremendous bulk of investment in all the most advanced parts of the economy. If this is true, and I think it would be most difficult to deny it, in a sense Norman Mailer was right when he said that we have not had prosperity, we have had a fever.

The fever involves, of course, a great deal more than the great corporations. It would be a grave mistake to consider it as the creation of a few people on the boards of the two hundred largest companies. We have a defense budget which deeply affects the interests of labor throughout the United States, and there is no need to remind any Senator or Representative of the importance of defense facilities or contracts to his district. We have the involvement of all of those rising new classes built on education and technology. And we have an important system of income transfers within the United States under which poor people seem to be subsidizing rather well-to-do people.

The question I pose, therefore, is whether our massive defense budget expresses a way of dealing with foreign problems or whether it reveals a way of preserving a certain pattern of life in the United States, a way of avoiding confrontation with domestic problems we have never solved. The most obvious of these is, of course, race. I wonder whether the military budget keeps us from spending what we must to equalize conditions within the United States, or whether, in fact, we hold on to the military budget because it gives us an excuse to avoid confronting ourselves as individuals and as a society with the real consequences of achieving something called equality.

Now, this is a question we have always solved on the frontier, and for that reason I suppose it is appropriate in some sense that we still seek its escape on the frontier—except that now our frontiers have moved on to the Mekong.

Do we have a national purpose—a purpose for national existence? It seems obvious to me that one of the reasons we hold on to the shibboleths of anti-Communism is simply because if we gave those up we wouldn't know what else to do. It is not an accident that the great fear and hue and cry about Communist China arose immediately after the test-ban treaty, when it seemed that we were going to solve at least some of our problems with the Soviets. We took five-year-old statements by Mao Tse-tung about the inevitability of conflict and raised them to the level of the greatest threat in the world, when it was Marshal Malinovsky who only two years before had been telling us that nuclear war was not inevitable and that there would be survivors.

All of us would agree that there is certainly something terribly unbalanced in our policy. We all recognize that the military budget is swollen. But we must do more than continue to tell ourselves that the magnitude of the threats has been obscenely magnified and that the quality of our response has been monstrously disproportionate. The question is, what are we going to do about it? Rather than asking who or what the Chinese or Vietnamese or Russians are, we must ask who the Americans are, and what kind of country this is, and what it is in our society that is leading us further in this direction.

II

Vietnam and Future Foreign Policy

The killing in Vietnam goes on. The war must be ended, and at the earliest possible date. We have put more than half a million troops in South Vietnam but have been unable to beat down the opposition of the North Vietnamese and the Vietcong. Dr. George Wald has said they have a secret weapon: they are more willing to die for their cause than we are to continue killing them.

The Vietnam war is destroying that unfortunate country and eroding the foundations of our society as well. Even our military position has been undermined. As General William Wallace Ford has noted, "The war in Vietnam has divided our people and weakened our military strength because of that division. You cannot create disenchantment among nearly all the youth of the country and expect to have a strong military posture."

Public discussion of the war or peace aims of the United States, or of the relationship this country will have to Southeast Asia when peace comes, remains obscured by obsolete and empty rhetoric. It is time to begin specific consideration of our national security interest in that area of the world. If the President is truly interested in negotiating an end to the war, such a discussion will help him, since one cannot reverse the set of assumptions on which our entire policy has been based without broad public debate.

If Congress is to make a responsible contribution to ending the Vietnam war, it must unshackle itself from the erroneous assumptions and faulty judgments of the past. Any viable political settlement in Vietnam will require a change in the underlying premises of the war, not a mere alteration in tactics. We must recall that it was the United States which, in contravention of the Geneva Accords of 1954, helped to create and sustain a separate South Vietnamese state and chose the leadership of that state. At this point our primary national interest is in extricating ourselves from Vietnam. The present military leaders in Saigon, however, have a personal interest in continuing the massive American military presence in Vietnam and are reluctant to see genuine progress toward a settlement that would allow our complete withdrawal.

As a result of past American policies in support of this military leadership, most non-Communist South Vietnamese are without political representation and are prevented from working out their own accommodation with the National Liberation Front. Many of the moderate political leaders of South Vietnam are in jail. Meaningful negotiations cannot go forward unless these currently unrepresented elements participate in working out the settlement.

The creation of a coalition government for South Vietnam must be considered as a necessary transition stage, and a possible model for the final settlement achieved through national elections or a referendum held under the aegis of the interim transitional coalition. This transitional stage has been neglected in most public discussion, but it is a vital period if the government which emerges from the settlement is to be a lasting one. It is manifest that neither the Saigon government nor the NLF trusts the other to carry out an election, and an initial period of shared power must precede any elections for a permanent government. An interim coalition could also maintain basic administrative functions while foreign troops are being withdrawn.

If we are not to find ourselves drawn into more Vietnams, the national security institutions that led us into the present quagmire must be reshaped and refocused. A new foreign policy must be evolved. Our national defense policy must be built around those core interests that are so vital that if they were violated they would threaten the very existence of the nation itself. In areas removed from our own interests, we can afford to seek or support settlements based on neutralization or on internationally agreed-upon solutions that will avoid big-power intervention and eventual conflict.

Many of the "threats" against which we maintain military forces exist not where a core interest of the United States is at stake, but because we have taken a particular historic position in a particular part of the world (as, for example, in Berlin and Korea). We must now reconsider the extent to which the maintenance of these positions is appropriate. It is questionable, for instance, that our decision to defend the Vietnam demarcation line ever had any validity in the face of the Geneva Agreement, although that agreement has been used to justify our military intervention.

American policy-makers have tended to believe that policies which were successful in one era can be applicable in all places at all times. The apparent success of the policy of containment in Europe after World War II led us to believe that containment would also be successful in Vietnam, the Middle East, and elsewhere. But relations between the major powers have changed so radically, and conditions elsewhere are so different from those in Europe, that entirely new perspectives are necessary. In particular, a policy directed to maintaining the *status quo* in the name of containing Communist influence is futile. We have learned that internal forces control the development of new nations to a far greater extent than any factors over which we or the Soviet Union have control. We must now accommodate ourselves to this realization and remove the vestiges of our earlier misunderstanding of the United States' role in the world. The defense establishment permitted military commitments overseas to evolve by making small, incremental decisions which then developed a momentum of their own, involving us ever more deeply in internal disputes beyond our control. We can no longer permit military perspectives to obscure our perception of political realities. A basic alteration in our policy of intervention and foreign military commitment is needed to correct the results of past mistakes and to prevent new ones.

Many of our overseas installations were created to serve

military needs that no longer exist. But the Defense Department has developed new rationalizations for keeping these bases—particularly the argument that it is desirable to maintain an American military presence as a foundation for political influence. But, recognizing the world-wide drive for national independence and greater democracy, we do not want our primary relationship defined by military bases or advisory missions. Our interests would be better served if the bases and the military advisers were gone.

Congress must force this re-examination of past commitments if any branch of government does. But to do so it must be informed of executive-branch decisions and must help to shape or halt them. Executive secrecy in the initiation of new American interventions is futile and self-defeating; Congress must insist on full, open, and current information, and must create mechanisms for reviewing our foreign commitments.

Congress must also insist that we begin to reduce the number of men in our standing Army to a level more suited to peacetime. Few world situations are imaginable in which this country would not have adequate time to build from its large reserves and enormous productive capacity should danger arise. The constantly accelerating rise of technological capabilities, and the maintenance of enormous armies which sit around waiting for a crisis to occur, are themselves important elements of instability and a prime cause of conflict. We should take into account not only the risk of war, but also the need, in Senator William Saxbe's term, to "take a gamble for peace." We cannot guarantee that disruptions will not occur somewhere in the world to which we cannot instantly respond, but there are other needs for our resources and more effective, multilateral approaches which we can use to advance the cause of peace.

Professor Neal: If the purpose of foreign policy is to enhance a nation's security and increase its well-being, then surely the foreign policy of the United States since the end of World

War II has failed. Today we have less security than ever. We have been engaged in repeated military adventures. We are bogged down in a war ten thousand miles away for aims we cannot define and which we can neither win nor end. We have become entrapped in a gigantic military-industrial complex that is bleeding us to death financially. We have dissipated much of the international trust and respect that was once ours. And we are beset internally, as a result of all this, with a deep social malaise which threatens our most cherished institutions.

There can be no way out of this situation until we reexamine the fundamental assumptions which underlie American foreign policy, and reorient that policy in directions that are more likely to enhance our security and well-being. Three major assumptions of our foreign policy are most at fault.

First is the assumption that the Soviet Union, by its very nature, poses a continuing threat of physical military aggression. The error here is compounded by the considerable confusion in our minds about the relationship between the Soviet Union as a state, Communism as an ideology and system, and revolution in general. The fact is that Soviet ideology, far from committing the U.S.S.R. to military aggression, either for national expansion or expansion of Communism, commits it *against* such action. According to Lenin's concept of "objective conditions" of revolution, it is both impossible to foment a revolution in the absence of such conditions and wrong to make the attempt.

Because Stalin, following Lenin's ideas, held that objective conditions for revolution were not present, Soviet policy in his time, no matter how uncooperative and unfriendly, was always inward-looking, defensive, even isolationist. The extension of Soviet influence into Eastern Europe—resulting from the Red Army's defeat of the Germans—is usually the evidence cited as proof of Soviet military aggressiveness. It was, in a sense, a type of political aggression, but certainly not physical military aggression in the sense we have been taught to fear it. Our first major policy effort based on this fear, the Truman Doctrine, sought to save Greece from Soviet Communist domination. As has now become known, Stalin not only did not support the Greek revolution but actively opposed it.

With the new doctrine of coexistence evolved under Khrushchev, the Soviet Union began to display an active, offensive foreign policy—based on Stalin's idea of supporting nationalist movements of all kinds—but at the same time was committed to the idea that *détente* with the United States was necessary to avoid thermonuclear war, not because the Soviet Union was especially "peace-loving" but because it was decided, wisely, that this was necessary for the interests of Communism and the U.S.S.R. It is necessary also, I think, for the interests of democracy and the United States.

Despite these facts, the whole direction of American foreign policy since the end of World War II has been based on the notions that we face a constant threat of Soviet military aggression and that the Soviet Union is committed to the physical destruction of the United States. We now seem ready to repeat the whole process in regard to China. This assumption about the danger of military aggression from the Communist states has permeated our whole social fabric.

The second assumption we must re-examine concerns containment. Two aspects of it are particularly erroneous and harmful: one, that we could restrain the spread of a political doctrine by military means and that revolutions everywhere were Communist-inspired and thus constituted a danger to the United States; and two, that we could deny to other great powers—like the Soviet Union and China—the extension of their influence beyond their borders without producing conflict. Another erroneous aspect of our idea of containment is the notion that the United States could always maintain clear and meaningful military superiority over the Soviet

Union. That has long since been demonstrated not to be the fact.

This leads us to the third assumption requiring re-examination, which concerns nuclear weapons. In the early postwar years, we began—against the advice of all the nuclear scientists, including even Edward Teller—to base our foreign policy on the idea that we could maintain our monopoly of nuclear weapons. When we saw that this failed, we believed we could obtain security through overkill and the balance of terror. It is now clear that the United States cannot achieve either security or political advantage from its continual efforts to gain superiority over the Soviet Union in thermonuclear weapons and missiles. The U.S.S.R. will always seek to overcome our superiority, and, in the future as in the past, it will be able to do so.

The Soviet Union long ago achieved parity in nuclear strength in any meaningful sense with the United States, regardless of how much overkill we have. Those who always insist we should not negotiate except from a position of strength are usually the same ones who, when we have such a position, either argue that negotiation is unnecessary or attempt to use it to impose on the U.S.S.R. a position of permanent inferiority. This gambit has not succeeded in the past and cannot succeed in the future, however devoutly we might wish it. Real negotiations are possible only on a basis of equality and in a spirit of mutual compromise. We cannot have them until we decide that the risk of constant escalation is greater than the risk of those substantive political agreements with the Soviet Union which are necessary for arms control and disarmament, without which there can be no real security.

The *reductio ad absurdum* of our failure to re-examine these faulty assumptions, the *reductio ad tragedium* of our policy, is the present morass in Vietnam. Without a re-examination of them, we are not only unlikely to extricate ourselves from Vietnam but also unlikely to avoid either further Vietnams or the catastrophe that is inevitable with endless arms escalation.

A re-examination of the underlying assumptions on which our foreign policy is based would, I think, indicate the desirability of a foreign policy reoriented in four major ways:

One—Our foreign policy should base itself on the idea of coexistence. This means primarily accepting the territorial *status quo* and the balance-of-power *status quo* among the thermonuclear powers. It would mean that we would seek stability in Europe by accepting the results of World War II as concerns a divided Germany and its borders. It would involve, also, acceptance by the Soviet Union and East Germany—as well as West Germany—of some kind of independent status for West Berlin.

Two—Our policy should be reoriented to the concept of core interests: those interests which a state regards, rightly or wrongly, as so vital to its existence that if they are threatened it will react as though the state itself were threatened. Core interests of smaller powers may be limited to territorial integrity. In the case of more powerful states, core interests invariably extend beyond their borders, although they are traditionally limited by geographic proximity.

The essence of foreign-policy formulation is the formulation of core interests which are within the capacity of a nation to assert. But this requires an understanding also about the core interests of other states—particularly pertinent for the United States in regard to Eastern Europe and Southeast Asia, and for the Soviet Union in regard to Latin America.

Three—There should be a reorientation toward the concept of neutralization. Many areas of the world are not clearly core interests of any great power, and the uncertainty often spells great danger. Along with international understandings about core interests should be international understandings about which areas of the world could be neutralized, which areas the great powers would pledge themselves not to intervene in. This is especially pertinent in the Middle East and Africa, but it could well be considered also for such an area as Southeast Asia.

There is, of course, no absolute assurance that we can reach international understandings on these matters. But certainly we cannot if we do not try. As George Kennan said about our policy on Germany, "You cannot tell whether the Russians will go through an open door until you stop trying to push them through a closed one."

Four—Finally, our policy should be reoriented toward the principle of internationalism. The United Nations cannot work so long as fundamental and serious conflicts persist between the United States and the Soviet Union. But while we try to resolve such conflicts, we should, jointly with the Russians—for there is no other way—seek cautiously to expand the scope of the independent authority of the United Nations Secretariat and, in particular, the role of the Secretary General as a mediator in all international conflicts.

We should also consider the desirability of channeling the bulk of our foreign aid through the United Nations. Most of our foreign aid has been down the drain and without results, in my opinion. Without strings it is squandered; with strings it produces only hostility. In addition, it has been amply demonstrated that the United States lacks the knowledge and understanding of foreign cultures sufficient to utilize its aid so as to contribute to development and stability. Even if we had to finance all or most of the U.N. aid ourselves, we should consider whether or not our foreign aims would not be better served if the United Nations administered foreign aid than if we did ourselves. Ultimately, reorientation to internationalism might produce a United Nations that was an effective peacekeeping agency in the areas of agreed-on neutralization.

Only if we reorient our foreign policy in these directions, in my opinion, can we hope even to approach meaningful security, and only in this way can we most advantageously serve our country and its ideals. If we can do it, then perhaps the world can relax, we can remedy the serious failings in our own society, and the United States can once again take its rightful place as the haven for peace and freedom and the well-being of mankind.

Professor Morgenthau: We have a tendency to assume that military and political successes achieved in one period of history will be applicable to all places at all times. In a sense, the successes of the policy of containment, of the Truman Doctrine as originally applied to Greece and Turkey, and of the Marshall Plan have become the curse of our foreign policy. Since containment was successful in Europe, we were led to believe that it would also be successful in the Middle East, Vietnam, etc. But the conditions that existed twenty-five or twenty or ten years ago have radically changed. Thus certain military policies which may have been sound twenty-five or twenty or ten years ago must be critically examined today in the light of entirely new circumstances. This applies particularly to the problem of revolution.

We are living, for better or worse, in a revolutionary period characterized by prerevolutionary conditions. The choice before us is therefore not between supporting a *status quo* which pleases us and opposing a revolution which displeases us, but rather between two different types of revolution. Either the revolution will be Communist-led against the United States, or it will be led by other forces—forces not hostile, at least, to the United States.

I should say in passing that considerable segments of the Catholic Church in Latin America have been able to grasp this basic fact and act accordingly.

We, on the other hand, have devised clever schemes going by the name of "counterinsurgency" by which we have tried to suppress and forestall revolution. We have transformed ourselves from what was once the revolutionary nation *par excellence* into a replica of Metternich's Austria, which from 1815 to 1848 tried to stifle liberal revolution. In consequence, we have applied to a revolutionary situation simple-minded and doomed military policies. For instance, we have completely misunderstood the character of the Castro revolution in Cuba, thinking that Castro was just another Latin American dictator superimposed upon an unwilling people and supposing that a thousand poorly armed emigrants landing in Cuba would overthrow him. Similarly, we still seem to believe that all that is needed in Vietnam is a series of so-called military successes over the Vietcong, and that a government which we installed in Saigon will somehow rally the people to its colors.

Finally, I think we have in good measure abdicated our own common sense and judgment in the face of so-called military expertise. I personally know absolutely nothing about electronics, but I claim to have common sense—if you wish, political judgment—as to the particular operations of the ABM or other military hardware. The really important question, the really decisive questions in the field of military technology are not scientific or technological; they are political. When it comes to political judgment, you and I are as well qualified to pass judgment as the so-called experts.

Here is a practical point which members of Congress ought not overlook—a point on which they have tended to abdicate in the past in the face of so-called expert judgment: even if we don't know anything about the technological intricacies of certain military hardware, we still know what the likely consequences are when it comes to decisions concerning military hardware.

Mr. Goodwin: If we are to accept the concept that military judgments are based on private information available to only a few people, we are trapped to begin with. Although classified information may be critical in certain rather specific cases, on the major decisions it seems to me that it is almost always irrelevant. For example, whether or not we maintain forces in Europe is basically a political-diplomatic decision and is not based on day-to-day secret information about the intentions of the Soviet Union—not on any information that isn't generally available to Kremlinologists. Whether or not we want to be able to move large forces from place to place, to combat revolutions in the Dominican Republic or insurgencies in Lebanon, is a decision based not on classified information, but on a general political judgment.

So there is much information that should be declassified; it has no particular reason to be classified. This includes much of the information about the intentions of the Soviet Union and what weapons the Soviet Union has. Presumably they know what they have, so they would not be learning anything. It is argued that in declassifying this information, the government might reveal a source of intelligence. But about eighty per cent of our sources are probably technological, and the technology of satellites and comparable devices is well known to them. Only in unusual cases are we forced to hold something back for fear of revealing a source.

Another important point about classified information is that it is often wrong, and one of the reasons it is wrong is that it is classified and therefore not subject to the kind of debate and discussion and contradiction and challenge which brings us closer to the truth.

I was for five years in the executive branch, about three and a half of those years in the White House. I attended many National Security Council meetings. I rarely learned a fact—other than a technological sort of fact—that would have changed any basic political judgment. I did hear and read intelligence estimates for years "proving" that we were going to win in Vietnam—classified information. I did read intelligence estimates that the Cuban people were rising in rebellion against Castro when the exiles landed. In the campaign of 1960 the Defense Department made available to the

Democrats, in a not unusual fashion, classified information showing the existence of a "missile gap" which did not exist.

I am not saying the people who prepared these things didn't do so in good faith. But the very fact that the information was limited and classified often made it erroneous, and the fact that it was classified had nothing to do with whether or not it was accurate and true. It just put a seal on it.

There was a scientific study of intelligence-gathering in Vietnam at one point, looking at how this intelligence was gathered in the field. It was found that many of the methods were so questionable that figures on infiltration from North Vietnam and that sort of thing could be off quite easily by four hundred or five hundred per cent.

So I do think that most major decisions can be made without access to classified information, and that except in the most extraordinary cases of national security, such information must be declassified if the democratic process is to work.

Professor Kahin: I have in mind another issue in military decision-making—those small, incremental decisions that develop a momentum of their own and finally a thrust so substantial as to make major decisions necessary in a context where the options have become very limited.

I am concerned with the capacity of the military to determine where the "threat" exists, and its inclination in many instances to undertake pre-emptive moves which later result in magnified problems. Small decisions, often made privately by a few, can later produce situations calling for a much larger American involvement than was initially perceived.

I could cite a whole catalog of live and dangerous situations in Southeast Asia, all attributable to decisions made without the minimally necessary knowledge of relevant political factors—decisions made, as far as I know, without Congress knowing about them and decisively counterproductive to immediate or long-term American interests. Just a couple of examples will suffice. There was the ill-fated introduction of Chiang Kai-shek's forces into Burma. I think it is not clearly realized that there is a considerable residuum of that problem in Burma, where this has given a fillip to tensions and to centrifugal political forces involving relationships between the political center and minority ethnic groups with whom those Kuomintang Chinese forces have linked up and whom they have supplied with arms. The problem also persists in Laos, where there is a substantial Chinese military element, and in northern Thailand, where around twelve hundred square miles of Thai territory are now under the *de facto* administration of Kuomintang troops.

Another instance is the United States' decision to transport large numbers of Cambodian South Vietnamese, trained with our special forces and with the South Vietnamese army, across Cambodia to the Thailand frontier where they regularly mount incursions into Cambodian territory. The logic of this is hard to understand, although I have heard a number of uniformly disturbing explanations.

Clearly, if Congress is going to play a responsible role in the field of foreign policy, it has to be advised of situations like this, where small decisions taken by a few American military and civilian officials add up to problems which become unmanageable and which take a quite different direction than initially perceived. I would submit that Congress cannot afford to remain willing, as it has been, to obtain its information on such situations from the activists whose decisions created the situations in the first place.

Representative Brown: It seems to me that we justify our large military presence around the world in terms of rather specific issues. In the case of Europe, for example, we still maintain that the long-standing failure to solve the central issue of Central Europe, the German question, poses a continuing threat to stability—the threat of an East German or Communist-bloc effort to take over West Germany. We used that to justify NATO and the large American military presence in Europe, including the bases, which admittedly are probably obsolete in terms of the original theory.

Nevertheless, we conceive of a threat to our basic interests in Europe in this failure to solve the German problem. This is not a threat to America *per se,* to the U.S. homeland. It is a threat to our commitment to protect West Germany and prevent any expansion on the part of the Warsaw Pact powers.

We are hung up in Asia over similarly divided countries. This is essentially the basis for our involvement in Vietnam. It was the direct basis of our involvement in Korea. We still perceive dangers in our failure to solve these critical political problems. So the military, because the dangers are said to exist, use them as a continuing basis for an expansion of their control over resources. We need to arrive at an understanding of whether these are actual threats to the United States or whether they are merely threats to positions we have taken which may or may not be valid any longer. I am not at all sure that our position to protect the Vietnam dividing line was *ever* valid. In fact it went in the face of the Geneva Accords. But, nevertheless, it is the excuse we use.

How do we resolve this? The one answer that occurs to me in Europe, for example, is: We recognize that our military contingent there is more or less a token contingent, that it couldn't stop the Russians but that, by being there, it perhaps has a psychological value. Why couldn't we move forward to a position where we say there would be even greater psychological value in an internationalized force under unitary command? Then, if the threat exists, if it is real, and if it were to manifest itself in a land invasion—and these are dubious assumptions anyway—the enemy would run over not just an American force but an internationalized force.

Professor Falk: One important consideration underlying many of our existing commitments and exemplified, of course, in Vietnam is the role we have assumed our military power can play with regard to revolution in the third world. The task of readjusting our commitments to our capabilities will require much greater awareness that our military power is largely irrelevant, if not actually harmful, to our aims and purposes in the third world—that we do better, in other words, when we do nothing. In looking around the world, one finds that in the few places where convulsive changes have seemed to promote American geopolitical interests (Indonesia, Algeria), these changes have come about not through American military intervention but largely because of its absence.

In Southeast Asia, for instance, one result of the American military presence has been to crystallize and coalesce an opposition to the entrenched forces that are survivors, to varying extents, of the colonial period. In Thailand, for example, prospects for political autonomy of a non-Communist variety have been seriously diminished (not promoted) by the American military presence, because there is now a neocolonial problem in Thailand that has united all radical opposition to the present established government; this is an ironic consequence of American foreign policy, since Thailand had never had a "colonial problem."

Professor Kahin: So far as the political facts of life in Vietnam are concerned, most of the American public—and, I'm afraid, a great many members of Congress—have been led by Alice through Wonderland for so long now that it is difficult for them to perceive the reality on this side of the mirror.

Congress simply must unshackle itself from the erroneous assumptions that have provided the rationale for the faulty judgments of those whose decisions brought this country to the present impasse. Certainly any reasonably viable political settlement in Vietnam requires a basic change in premises rather than a mere alteration in tactics and strategy.

The myths, I think, are well known: the allegation that what is basically a civil war is a case of outside aggression;

that an unpopular and narrowly based military oligarchy in Saigon enlists the support of a majority of the South Vietnamese people; and that the National Liberation Front is a puppet of Hanoi without significant popular backing in South Vietnam.

Surely, we shall sooner or later be obliged to recall that it is we who, in contravention of the Geneva Accords, helped to create and sustain a separate South Vietnamese state, and we who chose the leadership of that state that in turn invited us in to protect it. This is a matter of historical fact which may be politically embarrassing but which is part of the reality we must accept if we mean what we say about self-determination in South Vietnam. And genuine self-determination is a proposition we must be serious about if we are really interested in ending that war.

One must recognize that the military leaders who control the Saigon regime have a deep and vital interest in the continuation of a massive American military presence in Vietnam and in prolongation of the war. They will obstruct any genuine progress toward a negotiated settlement for as long as they can.

The Johnson Administration's uncritical support of Saigon against anti-Communist as well as pro-Communist opposition has narrowed and rigidified South Vietnamese politics, leaving only two polar extremes: the Saigon military leadership on one hand and the NLF on the other.

Since President Nixon has come into office, General Nguyen Van Thieu has been emboldened to move even further in eliminating all criticism of his regime, whether from non-Communists or from anti-Communist Buddhists. Within those (largely urban) areas actually controlled by Saigon, the majority of the population is politically voiceless and obliged to accept as its agent in any negotiation a military dictatorship which in fact it repudiates. Most non-Communist South Vietnamese are therefore cut off from working out their own accommodation with the NLF in accordance with their own best judgment of their interests.

An example of the general hardening of the South Vietnamese regime was the arrest on March 15, 1969, of the second-ranking Buddhist leader in South Vietnam, Thich Thien Minh, the head of the major Buddhist youth organization. He was sentenced to ten years at hard labor, which for him is tantamount to a death sentence. Two years ago, as a consequence of an assassination attempt ordered by Marshal Nguyen Cao Ky, he was nearly eviscerated. I should imagine that even a few months of hard labor will kill him.

It was divulged in a floor debate in South Vietnam's Senate late in 1968 that sixteen thousand new *political* prisoners had been arrested in the course of the year. The matter came up only because some Senators objected to the high cost of maintaining the jails. In response, the regime pointed out that many prisoners were held six or seven months before preliminary hearing, and this contributed to the cost of operating the jails.

If meaningful negotiations are to move forward, at Paris or elsewhere, the Saigon government must either be substantially broadened and made much more representative than it is, or it must be by-passed through some formula whereby currently unrepresented elements are given a significant role in working out a settlement—perhaps through some sort of autonomous negotiating authority. Any viable and lasting settlement must reflect political reality—the actual balance of political forces that obtains in the country. It seems to me, in that connection, that there has been great confusion about the concept of coalition government. This concept, as it applies to South Vietnam, must be discussed at two levels: as an interim transition stage in arriving at a final political settlement, and as a possible pattern for such a final settlement, achieved subsequent to nationwide elections.

Any forward movement in Saigon is critically dependent

on the political aegis under which it is undertaken. A temporary government coalition could provide a transitional bridge to elections and to a more broadly representative and enduring government, whether in the form of a coalition or not. But it is manifest that neither Saigon nor the NLF trusts the other to carry out an election alone, and therefore it will be impossible to by-pass an initial transitional period of shared power before the holding of elections or any other indication of the public will.

Thus the creation of an interim coalition government is not an end in itself; it is a means, a potential means. It would constitute an interim authority, whether alone or in conjunction with some neutral international presence, under which an expression of public will—an election or referendum or plebiscite—could take place. Such an expression of public will must be part of any process of self-determination. In addition, a coalition government could help maintain at least basic administrative functions throughout the country during the period of withdrawal of foreign troops and recruitment of indigenous military forces.

Senator Fulbright: I know your question is, "What can Congress do about ending the war?" Speeches can be made—isolated speeches—but it is impractical to think that any movement can be originated in Congress at the present time. I made a mild suggestion early in 1969 that time was running out, and the newspapers accused me of being impatient with the President. He ought to be given time, they said. This kind of approach makes it almost impossible to be effective.

I don't think we have the votes in Congress yet to do anything substantial about Vietnam. We have a new Administration with at least four years to go. We can try to carry the stick and complain a little, and then try to make up and see if we can persuade them, and alternate between the two in the hope of finding some way to influence movement.

I don't know what else to do. I can only say that I think

this is probably the calm before the storm. Unless something happens soon we face a bad time.

I have not detected any basic difference in the attitudes of the President, the Secretary of State, or the Secretary of Defense—any real acceptance of the kind of basic change in attitude toward Vietnam that Dr. Kahin says is necessary. The Administration still seems to be aspiring to what is vaguely called an honorable agreement, which I assume means the acceptance of our view that there must be a separate, independent, democratic South Vietnam dependent upon us. If that is still the goal, I think it will be difficult to achieve. But there is nothing to indicate that the Administration is ready to change the goal, or that it is ready to grasp the nettle and stop the slaughter.

Professor Galbraith: I would like to respond to my distinguished friend by pointing out that in the last year and a half, in the context of the war, when everybody is expected to rally to the flag, public opinion has executed an almost 180-degree turn. A strong anti-establishment, anti-institutional, and particularly anti-bureaucratic, anti-military mood is sweeping through the country much more rapidly than would have been possible as recently as ten years ago. This is partly because of the enormous number of people coming into the schools and high schools and universities, but also because of the large number of people who have been brought into our politics by the Vietnam war, and by McCarthy and McGovern and Robert Kennedy in 1968. These people have a far greater receptivity to ideas like those we are talking about than do most members of trade unions and political organizations, and far greater than the grain dealers and undertakers and other entrepreneurs who comprise the historic Republican rank and file. We have a responsive constituency running to millions in this country for the ideas we are discussing.

Senator Fulbright: Maybe I'm just disappointed. It seems incredible that a new Administration would come in after the experience of 1968 and after this long war and not want to change the policy immediately. What in the world are they waiting for? Perhaps there are good reasons. But one would think that after President Johnson's experience—and President Nixon is certainly an observer of the political scene—he would have concluded that this is not a profitable policy and that he wouldn't fool around with it.

Senator Saxbe: I would agree with Dr. Galbraith. I'm a little more optimistic than I was, and I assure Senator Fulbright that there are those on both sides of the aisle who admire his position and are trying to assist.

We came to the Senate with the attitude that Nixon was elected because of the war—that the war wrecked Johnson and that it would wreck Nixon unless he responded. Those of us who came in with this group believe our election was largely responsive to this national attitude. So we think we have more at stake than anybody else, because we came to Washington with a mandate to make ourselves heard as spokesmen for this public rejection of the war.

Representative McCarthy: I would like to address myself to the growing public concern about the military-industrial complex. I agree that public opinion is swinging to our side. But that doesn't make too much difference in Congress. When you look at the composition of the Armed Services Committee and the Defense Appropriations Subcommittee in the House, you find that some members tend to ignore public opinion. Faced with a choice, they would rather cut education and Medicaid, they would rather close hospitals, than reduce military spending. This is what you are dealing with. How do we change that?

Senator Nelson: We have been talking about how difficult it would be to change directions, to bring the so-called military-industrial complex under control; how difficult it is to find out what the military is doing and to get the Congress to do this and that. But we have ignored one significant factor: the youth of America, black and white.

The fact is that we will bring the military-industrial complex under control, or we will get a President and a Congress who will. The delay will not continue beyond the time when this generation starts to vote and to assume active leadership in the politics of this country—that is, the next six, eight, ten years. Members of Congress who are not prepared to undertake to do the job will not be re-elected. And it's starting right now.

We are reacting badly, as a country, to our young people. We run around asking, "What's wrong with the kids?" It isn't what's wrong with the kids; it's what's wrong with the country. They are reflecting what is wrong with the country, and what is wrong in every country—Yugoslavia, Czechoslovakia, France, Italy, Southeast Asia. The older folks say, "We can't understand the kids," but the kids understand their parents only too well. They understand the system, and they don't like it. They have good reason for not liking it. They are sick and tired of being involved in a war in Vietnam for which we have not yet figured out a purpose.

I remember hearing Dean Rusk say, time after time, "We have to contain China." There isn't a single Chinese soldier in Vietnam yet. Every time we gave a speech on that subject in the Senate, McGeorge Bundy would come over to counsel us "dissidents" and furnish another reason for the war. We cannot find a reason any more for being in Vietnam, and neither can the kids. They aren't going to kill people and get killed for no cause at all.

So in a handful of years we will manage the military-industrial complex, I think, all right enough. As the young people look at our institutions and the institutions of every other country, they see what we are doing to kill each other. They see we are expending vast sums in military enterprises that do not solve problems but create them. They see we are devastating the environment we live in—polluting the air, contaminating the water, killing the animals and birds, denuding the forests, destroying the beauty of the world. They

see all this and that it is all done in the name of "progess."
You could substitute the word "profit" and you would be more
accurate. The institutions we have created are destroying the
livability of the whole world, and the young people know it.
They may not articulate it well, but they sense it. They feel it.

The first issue raised by students in the past few years has
been Vietnam, because that is immediate and reflects their
rejection of the militarization of this and other countries. But
the second issue often raised is, "What are we doing to the
livability of the world? What are we doing to the air? What are
we doing to the water of the country? What are we doing to
the beauty of the nation?" So they are looking at what we are
doing, and rejecting the institutions that are doing it. Thank
heavens they are rejecting them.

But, we say, what they are doing on the campus is not related to what we are talking about. They can do on the campus
only what is within their jurisdiction to do. So they raise hell
with whatever part of the institution they can, because that is
where they are and that is where that institution is. The sooner
we understand that, the better off we will be.

I am much more optimistic than some of the rest of us
that the problems will come under control as soon as we throw
everybody out of office who is not interested in bringing them
under control. That will happen pretty soon—and the sooner
the better.

Professor Falk: I agree completely with Senator Nelson. One
way of expressing my agreement is to suggest that the *only*
positive effect of the Vietnam war has been to give the youth
of America an invaluable learning experience. Vietnam has
led the young to question why they are being asked to make
senseless sacrifices. But it has also provoked them to ask even
more fundamental questions which have started to discredit
both the institutional structure that exists in America and the
value priorities that have dominated our society in recent
decades—especially the imposition on a local community, and

on a society, and on a world, of values based on selfish economic and social considerations and on an obsolete image of national security derived from a prenuclear world.

I want to make an additional comment that relates to what Dr. Kahin said earlier about Vietnam and responds, in a sense, to what Senator Fulbright has said.

It is essential that the leadership of the country and the public in general understand one element in the process of settling the war in Vietnam: So long as a condition of the settlement is that it be acceptable to the present Saigon regime, the prospects for peace are exceedingly poor. The Saigon regime understands that it cannot survive peace, and it therefore has a maximum incentive to do everything possible to obstruct the settlement of the war.

Only when a phased withdrawal of American troops (fifty thousand to one hundred thousand every two months, with no specified terminal point) is indicated will there be leverage to persuade the Saigon regime to abandon its control or be overthrown, or to seek a bargain on its own. So long as Saigon retains the option of sustaining a military stalemate, the Thieu-Ky leadership has a maximum incentive to obstruct—and no incentive to cooperate—in the search for a negotiated settlement. So long as that option remains open, the United States government has virtually no leverage other than its presence in Vietnam with which to influence the Saigon government.

Therefore, Congress must assert these two points: first, that phased withdrawal is the only source of American leverage; and second, that such leverage must be used to reconstitute the Saigon regime in some manner that gives it a chance of surviving after a settlement. The political prisoners to whom Dr. Kahin referred must be released and given an opportunity to participate in the political life of South Vietnam without harassment. Third-force politics is the key to a political compromise in South Vietnam. Unless this issue is clearly presented and justly resolved, I just don't believe action is likely to take place within a reasonable period of time. To "de-Americanize" the war, as the Nixon Administration proposes, is to move in the wrong direction, encouraging rigid diplomacy on Saigon's part and equipping this isolated military government to fight against the majority of its own population, not just against the NLF.

Senator McGovern: On my way into the building I noticed an old car with a bumper sticker on it saying, "Let's build our model city with soul." That is what we need to do with the country. It is an open question whether we can continue allocating our resources to weapons of destruction and neglecting the kind of problems that Senator Nelson spoke about so eloquently, and maintain either our security or our soul as a country.

I would like to think we have learned some profound lessons from Vietnam. The only consolation I can find about that tragic war is that millions of people in this country have come to a new recognition of the limitations of military power, that they have come to understand that even a very powerful country cannot solve some of the crucial problems in the world, and that there are limits on what can be accomplished by simply piling up more and more weapons.

I think the second lesson we have learned is that military judgments are unreliable. Now there are reasons, of course, to be discouraged about how long it takes for that lesson to come across to many of our citizens and to our colleagues in Congress, but I share Senator Nelson's view about the rising tide of protest in the country.

I have great faith in what is happening among our young people today, and not just the young but all thoughtful people. Most of the Americans I talk with today think it is obscene that we are allocating so many of our resources to the military. Most of them long ago decided the war in Vietnam was a terrible blunder, that we ought to get out of it as soon as we can.

I think the question is whether, as Dr. Morgenthau has said, we can bring the mood of the country into an effective relationship with our political process. I don't know whether we will be able to do that. But if we can't, we are going to experience four years of unprecedented confusion and violence and despair in this country, and I tremble for its future.

III

ABM, MIRV, and the Nuclear Arms Race

The strategic balance between the United States and the Soviet Union, now at its most stable position in years, is about to be thrown askew. The United States is beginning to deploy an anti-ballistic missile (ABM) system and to install multiple independently targetable re-entry vehicles (MIRV) on its long-range missiles. Together, these will add to the arms race and create an environment of uncertainty and tension that will decrease our safety and make nuclear war an ever larger threat.

Today both the United States and the Soviet Union possess large, invulnerable strategic forces of nuclear weaponry. Each is confident that it has an effective deterrent to nuclear attack. Most Americans feel secure from the danger of nuclear war, and threats of nuclear bombardment such as were uttered during the late 1950s and early 1960s are no longer heard. Through improved satellite reconnaissance, each side is confident that it knows what strategic forces the other possesses, and each can assume that its own deterrent is secure from destruction in a surprise attack.

This relative equilibrium can be preserved through an agreement between the United States and the Soviet Union to refrain from constructing additional missile bases and from inaugurating ABM and MIRV deployment programs. Such an agreement could be an early result of strategic-arms-limitation talks between the two superpowers. The possibility that irrevocable steps will be taken before such an agreement is achieved lends

61

the gravest urgency to the initiation of those talks. Once large-scale ABM deployment begins and MIRV testing has been completed, the nuclear genie will be out of the bottle, and it is unlikely that the stability we now enjoy will be restored for many, many years.

We must attune our thinking to the realities of the nuclear age. We now imagine the worst that the Russians can do during the next decade, and then respond to what we imagine. We should instead forestall these further steps by an agreement which would halt what Robert McNamara called this "mad momentum" while there is still time. And while these talks are proceeding, we should delay deploying the Safeguard ABM system and halt the MIRV program. This will give us the last clear chance to stop the arms race.

Halting the nuclear arms race should be the first defense and foreign-policy goal of this country. Instead, we have been setting the pace in the arms race since the nuclear age began.

In the 1950s the United States, worried about Soviet aggression in Europe, developed the doctrine of massive retaliation. If Russia started a war through a ground attack in Europe, we would be the ones to start the strategic nuclear exchange with a direct attack on the Soviet Union. According to this scenario our missiles would reach the Soviet Union before theirs could get off the ground. This strategy required that we build many more weapons than the Soviet Union, since we could not be sure that each of our weapons would function properly and strike its target accurately. The Defense Department spent billions of dollars in an attempt to maintain such a first-strike posture.

To obtain the weapons for this purpose, the Defense Department fostered three different "missile-gap" scares. The first was in 1960. At a time when not a single Soviet intercontinental ballistic missile (ICBM) was deployed, this country was brought to near hysteria over the announced prospect that the Russians might have large numbers of missiles deployed within a very few years. Later we learned that by 1963 they had actually built only three per cent of the missiles that the Pentagon predicted they would have by that time, and they took seven years to close the missile-gap-in-reverse which we had opened up in the interim.

Then the impression was created by civilian officials in the Department of Defense that the Russians were building an ABM system throughout their country and that we had to increase the number of our warheads targeted on the Soviet Union to ensure that we could penetrate it. The result was the MIRV program. At a cost of more than five billion dollars, we are introducing new types of missiles with multiple warheads, each capable of being directed with high accuracy at a separate target. But it has now been revealed that the Soviet Union was not deploying an extensive ABM system after all, but stopped with a small (and now obsolete) system deployed around Moscow. Nevertheless, the MIRV program continues to move forward.

Most recently we have been presented with a third missile gap—involving the SS-9, a large Russian missile which the Pentagon is now describing as a first-strike weapon against our Minuteman force. In response to this newly discovered threat, based on an exaggerated description of the capacity of the SS-9s to threaten our ICBMs, we are told we must proceed with an ABM system. Since our ABM system will be at least ten times larger than the one the Russians have deployed, there will again be a gap in reverse.

The Defense Department has seized on the buildup of SS-9 missiles to argue that we must have a defense of our land-based missiles. But even without our land-based force, we would have a sufficient deterrent; each of our forty-one invulnerable Polaris submarines can destroy more than a dozen Russian cities and inflict awesome loss of life, not to mention the destruction which could be inflicted by our fleet of B-52 bombers and the tactical aircraft we have deployed around the world.

The Soviet Union has only a small fleet of missile-launching submarines at this time, and the Safeguard ABM system will diminish still further the effectiveness of this deterrent. Faced with the imminent threat of MIRVs and an American ABM system, the Soviet Union will have to multiply its missile force as quickly as possible if it is to maintain an effective retaliatory capacity.

The nationwide debate on the ABM has called attention to the dangers of deploying a system that will accelerate the arms race without providing greater security for anyone. However, the dangers of MIRV are not so widely appreciated.

With missile accuracy increasing, it will soon become possible for one missile, carrying up to ten independent warheads, to destroy several of the opponent's missiles on the ground. Either side can then, by striking first, destroy the other's offensive missile force *and* his ability to retaliate. To the extent that he relies on land-based missiles, his deterrent will be gone.

Compared with the ABM, the MIRV issue is an immediate one. The latter will take many years to be fully operational, but once MIRV is fully tested and deployable by either country, there will be no way of determining whether that country has deployed them, or in what numbers, and we can no longer have a self-policing arms agreement with the Soviet Union. The time to halt the MIRV program is in the test phase, which began in the United States in the fall of 1968 and is continuing.

We can halt the testing of MIRVs because we know that the Russians have not proceeded to deploy their ABM system, nor are they testing MIRVs. They have been testing multiple warheads, but theirs are not yet independently targetable. Since their warheads do not appear to have independent guidance, they do not pose a threat to our Minuteman missiles, which, protected as they are in underground concrete silos, must be attacked with high accuracy to be destroyed.

Our MIRV program began in response to a putative Soviet ABM system. Now that this Soviet ABM system no longer appears to be a significant threat, the Pentagon has adopted another, far more dangerous rationale for MIRV: that it will allow us to attack missile sites in the Soviet Union. The Defense Department thus wants to develop the very first-strike capability that we are told to fear from the Soviet Union. Just as we reacted with both missile and anti-missile deployments to the suggestion that the Russians might be building a first-strike force, so they will surely respond if we continue to seek such a capacity.

We should instead suspend our MIRV program by halting the flight testing of MIRVs, and we should consider resuming this testing only if it appears that the Russians are again pursuing an extensive ABM program. Testing of MIRVs intended for penetration of an ABM system would take no more than eighteen months, as compared to the five to seven years required to deploy an ABM system. We would know in the very early stages if the Soviet Union were going ahead with an ABM program, and there would be no danger that the Russians could achieve a significant lead.

The testing of MIRVs can easily be detected by unilateral intelligence. Long-range flight tests of ICBMs can be detected with radar and other devices, and multiple warheads can be seen as they descend. In addition, the extensive detection net in the target area used to determine the accuracy of individual warheads can be observed through reconnaissance satellites and other means. Thus, if we were to halt our MIRV testing and then agree with the Soviet Union that neither side would resume such tests, this would be a self-enforcing, easily policed agreement.

It is most important that the MIRV and ABM programs be halted while strategic-arms-limitations talks proceed. If the Russians perceive that we have developed the ability with MIRVs to destroy a substantial portion of their missile force in a first strike, they will not be willing to agree to halt the further buildup of their deterrent. Just as we cannot tolerate their achieving a first-strike capability, so they cannot permit us to achieve one. Simultaneously, the Soviet Union should be asked to halt deployment of its SS-9 missile. While the talks go on, there should be a moratorium on both sides. The fears expressed by the Defense Department regarding Russian capabilities involve possible developments in the 1970s; an agreement to halt the buildup now would insure that such fears could be put aside.

Security from attack depends today on preventing conflict, not on having the ability to win it. No one can win a nuclear war, and the existence of nuclear weapons must lead us to look beyond weapons to the more fundamental demands of our national security.

Professor Falk: We have consistently been overdesigning nuclear weapons systems on the basis of the most conservative possible estimate of what the other side's intentions might be under a most implausible set of circumstances. This logic of "defense" is communicated to our adversaries, who imitate it because they are somewhat behind us. They apparently feel that since we think this way they have to think this way too. The Soviet military budget has been consistently sensitive to increases and decreases in U.S. military spending.

That kind of logic at the strategic level assures a continuing dynamism in the arms race, with both sides overdesigning to cope with what they think the other side may be doing. This process might have been a tolerable luxury in the prenuclear age. It might even have been a tolerable luxury in the early years of nuclear technology. But today it leads to a dangerous kind of confrontation as these weapons systems escalate in their capabilities and decrease in the time needed for their delivery, and as the financial burden withdraws resources from other needs of the society and the world.

There is a parallel distortion of priorities in our heavy development of conventional weapons. Demands for superfluous resources generate a kind of political pressure to demonstrate that those demands are justified. The consequence is to encourage an interventionary diplomacy. We conceive of missions to justify earlier assertions that needs existed. A propensity to intervene arises out of the very argument that counterinsurgency capabilities are essential to national security.

I would argue therefore that the essential first step to getting this problem under control is to establish some sense

of what are the genuine security needs of the United States.
Professor Morgenthau: I don't think there is any difference
between my position and what one might call official ortho-
doxy insofar as national priorities are concerned. One can
take it for granted that the security of the nation is the first
priority, for if the nation is not secure in its existence, whatever we do by way of domestic reforms will avail us nothing.

The real problem arises when one asks what is needed
for national security. Here, indeed, we are confronted with
a mode of thinking which is obsolete and which has always
been too narrow to appreciate and correctly evaluate the
basic problems of national security. Military thinking, as it
still prevails in the main body of the military establishment,
is obsolete. It operates with categories appropriate for a
conventional war and completely inappropriate for nuclear
war.

Within the framework of conventional war, the arms race
was a perfectly rational instrument of national policy. The
more machine guns you had compared with your enemy, the
better off you were in this particular department. However,
when it comes to nuclear weapons, once you have reached
the optimum of being able to destroy your enemy a couple of
times over even under the worst of circumstances, the arms
race becomes a complete absurdity. Yet we are still practicing
the arms race with regard to nuclear weapons, unable to
understand this basic difference between nuclear and conventional weapons.

It has been said that throughout history each new weapon
has called forth a defense against it. That may have been
correct for conventional weapons. It is certainly incorrect for
nuclear weapons; for the destructiveness of nuclear weapons
is so enormous that it dwarfs all possible defenses. Your
aim must be not to defend yourself in a nuclear war, but
to prevent a nuclear war. If you have been unable to prevent
a war through deterrence, no defense will protect you.

General Ford: You cannot expect to escalate the ballistic missile or anti-ballistic missile or any other war weapon without having your potential enemy react, and it is utterly ridiculous to say that the building of a token ABM system is not provocative of further reaction by Russia.

The reasons given by the protagonists of the ABM sound a bit like the reasons given over the years for our presence in Vietnam. We were told this reason and that reason, and you could hardly put your finger on the reason before it moved. The story was that the ABM system was conceived as protection against the Chinese. Then the military said no, it was protection against Russian missiles, protection of our cities. Now it is for the protection of our ballistic missile sites. The excuses for these things do skip around.

There is no end to this. At best, we could escalate the arms race from now until eternity and sacrifice everything else our society hopes to gain to the enormous sums spent on weapons. At worst, of course, the holocaust.

Dr. Stone: The Department of Defense has become an inventor and a merchandiser of exaggerated fears. It has become an unscrupulous lobbyist to get the weapons to answer those fears. Worst of all, through the action-and-reaction phenomenon, its aggressive pursuit of the arms race has greatly undermined the security of the nation by unnecessarily stimulating Soviet efforts to keep up.

The Department of Defense has never been responsible for a serious effort to halt the arms race by negotiation. It has been extraordinarily complacent about many serious threats to our survival. It has traditionally taken the view that the only nuclear danger the country faces is premeditated Soviet aggression. It has taken the view that this danger could be resolved with certainty if only the United States bought every new strategic weapon that might conceivably work, and bought it in larger numbers than the Russians.

Meanwhile the survival of this country has fallen under a

cloud. We can now be destroyed in an hour as a result of unintended escalation—perhaps beginning with some incident on the German Autobahn. This is not a danger faced, say, by Brazil or Australia. And it was not faced by the United States twenty years ago. In the name of security the Defense Department has developed rules and ways of thinking that undermine security. There is a cost to buying too many weapons, and that cost is an uncontrolled arms race. I want to explain how that arms race works.

In the 1950s the accepted U.S. doctrine was massive retaliation. The United States was worried about Soviet aggression in Europe, and we were prepared to respond by attacking the Soviet Union directly. The Russians would start the war in Europe, but we would probably be able to attack Soviet missiles before they were launched against us. From that time on, and still today, the Defense Department has spent billions to give our missiles the ability to destroy Soviet missiles on the ground. Our strategic posture has in this sense always been a first-strike posture, not a retaliatory posture only. Every serious scholar of these matters knows this is so.

This policy requires far more weapons, and far more accurate weapons, than are necessary just to destroy Soviet cities in retaliation. In order to get the weapons, the Defense Department bureaucracy has created, permitted, encouraged, and fostered three different missile-gap scares in this decade alone.

First there was the missile-gap scare of 1960. The entire country was alarmed by exaggerated future estimates of Soviet missile production, even while U-2 planes showed clearly that the Russians had no ICBMs at all. Secretary McNamara admitted, in his famous September 1967 speech in San Francisco, that the United States had started far too many missiles in 1961. Spurred by the missile-gap fears, the United States had opened a missile-gap-in-reverse which took the Soviet Union five to seven years to close. In 1962 we began to build a missile per day, while the Russians were building only one per week. (They did not become capable of building one a day until 1967.) They did not catch up in numbers until we had shifted our emphasis to increasing the efficiency of each missile and therefore ceased for three years to increase the numbers of our missile launchers.

Next there was the anti-missile gap. The country was given the impression that the Russians might be building an "airtight shield" over the Soviet Union, requiring massive increases in numbers of U.S. warheads. The Department of Defense began to insist on increasing the number of targetable U.S. warheads from 2400 to 8000 or 10,000 by putting many missiles on each existing missile launcher. This is the MIRV program. Now the Deputy Secretary of Defense admits that the Soviet Union has made no commitment to a missile defense of any significance. Has the MIRV program been stopped? It has not. Instead, in the old pattern of strategic opportunism, the Department of Defense is openly putting high accuracy on the 8000 additional warheads so that they can be used to attack Soviet land-based missiles. And it is going forward with a missile defense that is bigger than Sentinel—one that will open an anti-missile gap in reverse.

Faced with a U.S. missile defense and this imminent threat of accurate multiple warheads, the Soviet Union must multiply its missile force as quickly as possible to maintain a retaliatory capability. The Soviet SS-9 missile, which can be given multiple warheads, is an efficient way to do this promptly. But the Defense Department has seized on the Soviet buildup of SS-9s as constituting a third missile gap, arguing that *our* land-based missiles may be attacked if the SS-9 ever gets anywhere near as accurate as we have already made our own missiles.

But we are in no danger whatsoever of losing our deterrent. With MIRV, we would soon have the ability to destroy *one hundred and sixty* Soviet cities with any one of our forty-one invulnerable submarines. The U.S.S.R. does not have one hundred and sixty cities. Nevertheless, the Department of Defense has seized upon the SS-9 as a threat to land-based missiles. And, in the same pattern of strategic opportunism, it has expanded the old Sentinel missile defense proposal so that these weapons might try to shoot down Soviet submarine-launched missiles—the only kind of Soviet deterrent that cannot be destroyed on land in an initial attack.

What is this Defense Department pattern? It is one of undermining the Soviets' deterrent while complaining that they may in the future undermine ours. The pressures in the Department of Defense go far beyond its traditional underestimate of the costs of American weapons and over-estimate of their effectiveness. The Department invariably exaggerates the Soviet threat to obtain public and Congressional support for weapons that will undermine the Soviet deterrent. This means a permanent arms race. Some counter-vailing pressure must be found. The size and zealousness of the Department of Defense now constitute a distortion in our society.

This is the last clear chance to do something about the arms race for several years. Once we have modified and completed our tests on MIRV and begun substantial deployment, it will be impossible for either side to know how many warheads the other side has on its missiles. There could be eight or ten at the top of the missile. Nobody would know. On a Polaris missile you could put ten; on the Minuteman, three. But you could put more or less. The Russians won't know whether we have ten thousand warheads or five thousand, or what.

If the Russians try to do the same thing, we won't know what they have on their warheads either. This is why former Defense Secretary Clark Clifford testified that "technological developments may well make any arms limitation agreement more difficult to develop and enforce a year from now than it is today." The two things we would hope to talk the Russians out of in the strategic talks, the two things those talks are about, the two things we would hope they do not do, are the very two things this Administration seems to be putting on the road irrevocably—the MIRV and the ABM.

I think it is worse than a disgrace to go past another point of no return when there is a real chance for stability, perhaps the best chance in twenty years. If there were a moratorium on both sides at this time, we would not have to worry about the SS-9. All the fears expressed are about the mid-1970s, but if things stop now there will be no need for this fear on either side. If they do not, and if the Defense Department continues in the same pattern, we will have a permanent arms race.

In my opinion much of the problem is that the Defense Department has no counterbalancing pressures resisting it. Some way must be found to confront a bureaucracy so large and entrenched, so zealous and so parochial, with opposing points of view.

Professor Schultze: I think Dr. Stone is eminently correct. There is a time-bomb limitation on the MIRV. In the long run the MIRV is much more important than ABM, at least the early stages of the ABM, where you are protecting missiles. The key problem with the MIRV is that once testing passes the point when the other side knows you can deploy them, you can no longer have a self-policing arms agreement. Hence, testing the MIRV seems to me a specific, explicit proposition, as important as, if not more important than ABM. Deployment is something you can hold off for a while, but, to the best of my knowledge, there is a time limit on testing which is fairly short-fused.

Dr. Stone: The reason we are in such trouble with the MIRV program is because of secrecy. This is an important object lesson. Nobody has been making loud public objections to the MIRV program, the way they have for years to the ABM.

The reason is interesting: When the Defense Department first thought of MIRV, its second thought was, "If the Russians got this they would be able to destroy our Minuteman missiles." So, Secretary McNamara directed that this had to be highly classified and that nobody should talk about it. As a result, the debate was shut off for three years while the program got under way.

Now, if you talk to Senators in the ABM fight and ask them to call for a stop on ABM *and* MIRV, they say to you, "Look, there has been no outcry about MIRV. We have problems already with the ABM. We can't take on both of these until there is public preparation for it."

The way to prepare this, if you want to do something sensible and urgent and timely, is to call for a halt in testing of the MIRV program. First, the Deputy Secretary of Defense has testified that the Russians have made no significant commitment to missile defense. Since the MIRV program's main rationalization was to beat down a Soviet missile defense whose lead time is at least as long as that required to deploy MIRV, we could fairly hold back on it.

Second, if we continue the tests, we will go past the point at which we can negotiate with the Russians about it. Third, the Administration concedes that the Russians are at least a couple of years behind us in MIRVs. If you look at the Pentagon fact sheet closely, they say the Russians are testing MRVs, not MIRVs. We already have multiple re-entry vehicles (MRVs) for our missiles. They don't pose the problems we have been talking about. But MIRVs, multiple *independently targeted* re-entry vehicles, which permit a missile to launch several little missiles at one missile site and another one at another site and another at another site with independent guidance and high accuracy—that is the problem we are talking about.

There is reason to believe that the Russians will never invest large sums to achieve very high accuracy on multiple warheads. If you cannot strike Polaris, there is no point in spending money to attack Minutemen even if you were seeking a way to strike first. They may never go into this technology in the way we have, just as they have not spent money for high accuracy on their Minuteman-type missile, the SS-11.

Senator Nelson: I understand it is relatively easy to discover deployment of a missile because of the size. How does our military know that if we stop deployment of the MIRV, the Russians won't proceed with it?

Dr. Stone: Testing of it is very distinctive. A missile goes up and five different projectiles can come out of it and they start going their separate ways. We sit around the Pacific and we see it.

Senator Nelson: Do you have the same guarantee that you would discover a test of MIRV as you would the deployment of ABM, for example?

Dr. Stone: I think you could detect both. I have prepared a report from public sources on the reconnaissance capabilities of the United States, and I can tell you that we can see, from satellite altitudes of one hundred and two hundred miles, not just dinner plates or garbage cans but telephone wires; although they are only an eighth of an inch wide, their length permits them to be visible on the films. The advances made in reconnaissance are enormous. Even missile sites with grass growing over them are evident to those who use other parts of the electromagnetic spectrum to find out where they are. This is why President Johnson and Secretary McNamara testified that we know exactly how many missiles the Russians have. I don't think there is a reconnaissance problem about almost anything nowadays—certainly not tests of MIRV— except deployed MIRVs *after* testing.

Senator Nelson: I am aware of what you said about the missiles, but I don't know enough about MIRV. Why is the testing of MIRV so conspicuous that you are sure you can catch the test in a matter of minutes? How are you so certain we will be able to observe that, as contrasted with the deployment of ABM, which is a big installation?

Dr. Stone: I want to say two things about that. First, since we have a two-year lead in MIRV we can invest a few months in negotiations, even if we can't be sure about MIRV. Second, you can tell where the tests are because they are visible. MIRV tests go on in the atmosphere, and these things fly out. You have to do a series of tests, not just one. The missile and its warheads show a visible, distinctive pattern.

Let me say that these first approximations to the inspection problem don't fully encompass all the ways we can inspect what the Russians do. I am not just talking about defectors and spies and listening in on telephone conversations as some of our satellites do—according to public sources. Even *after* you deploy these things you have to test them occasionally, because if you did not you would not know they were still working.

The point of no return that is being passed is a *political* point of no return. Strategically, we could put our faith in Polaris submarines. The fact is that Congress will not support an agreement in which it can't tell exactly how many warheads the Russians have, even if it did not matter strategically.

Professor Rodberg: The danger of MIRV, which Dr. Stone pointed out clearly, is that it can hit accurately at several different missile sites. To test the success of several independent warheads landing very accurately, you need an elaborate test set up on the ground to see where they are coming down. That kind of extensive test program can be observed by the techniques that he talked about and from ships and by a variety of other means.

Senator Nelson: Of course you could deploy MIRV without testing. You could go ahead and not test but deploy it to have whatever advantage it would give you.

Professor Rodberg: Then it would not be a reliable weapon because it would not have been tested for accuracy.

Professor Rathjens: I am not sure I would agree that the MIRV problem is more serious than the ABM. If we stop either we are in reasonably good shape. If we fail on both then I really do see a spiral in the arms race from which it will be hard to get off. We would get off eventually, but a hundred billion dollars further along, perhaps.

We can easily afford to stop the MIRV tests now. We have probably gone far enough already to deploy a system that would be adequate to penetrate defenses with almost no further testing. If you have a reasonable chance that a reasonable number will get through, that would be enough to cope with any ABM system the Soviet Union might employ—and we don't see any in evidence yet. You don't need the accuracy. You don't even need the reliability. I believe that we would lose little at this time if we had a moratorium on further testing—unless we are determined to go ahead and develop a pre-emptive first-strike weapon against Soviet missile forces. If we really want to do that, we have to go ahead with an extensive test program to achieve the necessary confidence in its reliability and accuracy.

I alluded to two motivations for the MIRV system: the desire to have a reliable means of penetrating a possible ABM system, and the desire for a counterforce capability. There is a third: Once somebody comes up with an ingenious idea like this, there is a tremendous technical challenge to bring it to fruition. I can understand the technical people wanting to do that, but I do believe that this is a case where the political leadership has to exercise its restraint.

Representative Rosenthal: How do you exercise that political restraint when you don't have the scientific and technical know-how to rebut the technicians?

Professor Rathjens: The problem is not in the technical details of the system, but whether or not MIRVs are needed. They are not. There hasn't been a need for quite some time. The day we ascertained that the Soviet Union was probably no longer going ahead with a nationwide ABM deployment was the day we should have decided to halt MIRV.

Representative Fraser: I think it is important for those of us who are not technically qualified to understand why a continuation of testing takes us past your point of no return. Why is it so significant? For members of Congress to say, "Quit testing before you are sure the system will even work"—that puts a substantial burden on us. I think we have to understand very clearly what arguments compel our taking that position.

Professor Schultze: Let me try my hand at this problem. If we were developing a missile that, once deployed, the Soviets could identify and count, the testing argument would not be critical. The particular characteristic of the MIRV is that once a nation deploys it on that covered warhead, there is no way to know how many have been deployed. Therefore the only way of reaching a self-enforcing agreement—self-enforcing in the sense that you don't just trust the other side to give you the figures but can tell what he is doing—is *before* the MIRVs are put on. How do you catch it before he puts it on? You can see his testing, you can determine what he is testing. If you are still in the position where he has not tested it to the point of being able to deploy it, there can be an agreement on testing; you can police testing of a MIRV system. Once the United States tests MIRV to the point where Soviet planners begin to have a large suspicion that we can deploy it, they will not agree to a moratorium, as we would not in a similar circumstance.

Professor Rodberg: This is not a case of stopping the advance of knowledge; this is testing something we know we can do. It is like designing a new car. You know you can design a new car; it just takes you eighteen months to two years to do it.

I would also point out that it takes between five and seven years to deploy a large-scale, or even moderate-scale, ABM system. It would take only eighteen months to develop a MIRV program from the day we decided to go ahead with it.

Professor Rathjens: A MIRV program for penetration of an ABM system. Not adequate for a first strike.

Professor Rodberg: Yes. Dr. Rathjens mentioned three possible reasons for going ahead with MIRV. The one that is beneficial from the point of view of deterrence is to be able to penetrate a Russian ABM system. For that purpose you don't need very high accuracy, as he said. You need to be able to disperse your warheads so that the ABM has many targets to face. There you have the disparity in time scales. Five to seven years for an ABM system and eighteen to twenty-four months for the MIRV. So holding off and watching for Soviet ABM progress does not endanger your chances of penetrating their ABM.

Professor Rathjens: If we were to contemplate a first strike against the Soviet Union we would want an extraordinarily high confidence that that system would work. Such a degree of reliability implies a program that probably involves firing several dozen tests.

The other problem is accuracy. It is quite clear that we don't have that accuracy yet. With the size boosters that we have, MIRVs would not be a useful counterforce weapon. A Minuteman missile is a better weapon with a single warhead than it is with multiple warheads if it is going to be used for counterforce purposes.

Professor Kistiakowsky: Once you put on multiple warheads, each warhead is much smaller and therefore has to hit much closer to the target to be effective.

Professor Rathjens: That is exactly right. It will take a long and exhaustive program to make MIRVs useful for counterforce purposes, and to this extent I would disagree with Dr. Stone. I don't think it is six months. I don't think it is that time scale at all. I don't think it is any billion-dollar program either. It will cost a lot more than that before we get to the point where these things are critical.

The other program, to get through ABM defense, is a quite

different thing. I would agree with Dr. Rodberg that it would probably take only eighteen months.

Dr. Larson: But doesn't even that less accurate MIRV raise the inspection problem we talked about—the self-enforced inspection problem? Wouldn't that still leave uncertainty on their side on what we have ready to deploy?

Professor Rathjens: Yes. I would agree. I don't see any other way of dealing with the MIRV problem than controlling it during the test phase, to avoid the kind of inclusive inspection agreement which I don't believe is going to be negotiable within the next decade.

Representative Leggett: It is my view that it would be a mistake to take a position against a specific thing like testing of MIRV at this time.

To begin with, we have concluded considerable testing on our multiple independent re-entry vehicles, to the point where we are now awarding contracts. We have awarded them for the Minuteman III and Poseidon. We have submarines in ports at the present time undergoing major overhauling to accommodate Poseidon. I was at Cape Kennedy not long ago, where Lockheed is developing Poseidon, which has a ten-plus independent vehicle capability. It has a system that is working.

I don't think it would be in our interest to come out at this time for a unilateral abatement of testing. I would hope that we could aim our deliberations more toward the ABM program. Maybe somewhere down the line we can take on numbers and sophistication of missiles and the type of garbage they put in the container that provides the chaff. There are a hundred different kinds of things that are needed. The reason the Soviet Galosh ABM system, which is two-fifths completed around Moscow at this time, has abated in the past year is that we have overtargeted and we have this multiple capability coming along.

I think it is important that we relate to the majority of Congress or to as large a number as we can, unless we want to be a voice for a powerless minority. Right now we are tasting some power. I think it important that we not weaken a potential majority by coming up at this time with too many things which people would be against.

For instance, the Poseidon program has considerable support, and it is already being installed in various ports around the country. You have to take on defense systems over a long lead time, and I don't really see anything magic that will occur over the next five months.

Representative Burton: How do you deal with the expressed concern that the Soviets, if they believed we have advanced our technology to the point where our MIRV system has first-strike capability, would be less willing to enter into a meaningful disarmament agreement with us?

Representative Leggett: The Soviets know that we have tested MIRV and are in the process of constructing it. This is worth discussing in arms limitation talks, but since we are ahead of the Soviets with a MIRV that is virtually developed, they won't stop their testing while they discuss arms limitation. Considering that, I don't think we ought to make a statement advocating a halt to the MIRV program. Inevitably we have to get some limitation on numbers of missiles, the kinds of garbage that go with the missiles—the decoys, the other kinds of chaff they create. But I don't think this group should advocate that we do that without any reciprocity on the part of the Soviet Union.

I am not a unilateral disarmer. I call myself a cheap hawk, and I like the nation to be as strong as it can be within the framework of a reasonable budget.

Professor Rathjens: It seems to me that the boat was missed in August 1968. I don't think there is any realistic possibility now of bringing the MIRV program to a halt unilaterally. On the other hand, it does seem to me that if we were to carry on negotiations with the Soviet Union leading to their agreement not to deploy a nationwide ABM system, there would then be a great deal of leverage available to those who want to stop the MIRV program. Indeed, it would probably be a necessary part of the agreement. If we do not begin the negotiations soon, however, they will be fruitless either because of the ABM problem or because of the MIRV problem, or both.

Professor Schultze: I want to second what Dr. Rathjens has said, and try once more to underline the urgency of the combined MIRV-ABM negotiation problem. Again I come back to the point that time is of the essence.

In his testimony before the Senate Armed Services Committee in which he shook the Soviet rockets at us, Secretary Laird asked for additional money for the Poseidon program for the following purpose, and I am quoting from his testimony: "This is an important program since it promises to improve significantly the accuracy of the Poseidon missile, thus enhancing its effectiveness against hard targets." To the extent that that goal is achieved, the United States will possess, just with Poseidon alone, anywhere from four thousand to six thousand hard-target killers.

Put yourself in the position of the Soviets and ask yourself, "What kind of meaningful disarmament agreement am I willing to sign when the other side is well along the road and possibly past the point where I can further check it?" Not two hundred hard-target killers or even eight hundred, but four thousand to six thousand on Poseidon missiles alone.

Perhaps Dr. Rathjens is right when he suggests tying this issue to the urgency of immediate negotiations. But I think we would be kidding ourselves if, in talking about the long-term need to gain political support and a favorable national view about priorities, we delayed and got ourselves locked in.

Representative McCarthy: I am disturbed by what Dr. Rathjens and Dr. Schultze have just said. Here we are, members of Congress who should know these things. But I don't think the full impact of MIRVs came home to me until just now.

This is of the greatest importance. We have had peace in

the nuclear age because both the United States and the Soviet Union had the power to retaliate, which made a first strike irrational. This is the nuclear balance in the world today. Now, both the Soviets and ourselves are on our way to achieving a first-strike capability. This is of critical importance to the peace of the world. I would heartily endorse the recommendations of Dr. Rathjens and Dr. Schultze that we put the highest priority on the need for prompt and early discussions with the Soviet Union. We may have reached the point of no return in a matter of months.

Dr. Stone: It isn't enough to call for prompt talks, because everybody knows that the talks may take several years. The proliferation treaty negotiations—for a far simpler treaty—took a long time too. What *is* necessary and politically feasible to ask for at this point is a stand-still halt on both sides. This removes the onus of a unilateral stoppage.

The best way to protect us is to call for a three-year moratorium and propose that the negotiators draw up a written agreement during that period which both sides could sign and which would last for a longer period.

From a strategic point of view, the real question is MIRV plus ABM together. Unless they are both stopped at the same time, either one going forward will shake the whole strategic situation like jelly. Everything is so related nowadays that you cannot have stability unless you bring everything to a halt. To focus on the ABM issue *alone* is to assume that you can kill ABM, but you cannot. You can only defer it. We have deferred it for ten years. But we cannot do more than defer it, because it stays in research and development. The only way to kill it is to have an arms-control agreement. Without the arms-control talks and moratorium, the ABM will be back again. That is why these things have to be linked together.

Mr. Goodwin: I think it is clear that once either side assumes that the other has a first-strike capability, the deterrent strategy of the last twenty-five years is gone. The incentive to attack will obviously be far greater than it was before, because if you think the other man can knock you out and you won't be able to retaliate, it will take much less tension for you to conclude you had better hit first.

If *both* sides in fact develop a first-strike capability, that would lead to the most volatile situation of all. Then the temptation and pressure on each side to knock the other out would be tremendous. This is much more than another dangerous weapons system. It creates a situation that threatens to destroy the one thing—the deterrent philosophy—which has provided some restraint on nuclear war.

My own judgment about this is that we are faced with a political issue. Obviously we are not going to change the minds of the Joint Chiefs of Staff. I doubt that we will change the mind of the Secretary of Defense. But we may be able to reach the President and the Congress if, in fact, there is strong popular feeling on the ABM issue specifically and on the military issue generally.

The ABM issue was, in a sense, a gift. The mistake, unrelated to the system the Pentagon was trying to set up, of situating anti-ballistic missiles around major cities—a decision which was not, so far as I know, in McNamara's original plan —gave many of us the opportunity to coalesce an opposition that could be heard. Now, even though some of the pressure is off because the ABM is not to be deployed around cities, it has become an issue important in itself, but also symbolic. If you could win it politically, it would open the door and demonstrate for the first time that you can challenge a weapons system. It would give added support and strength to many members of Congress and to people generally, and it would certainly give the Administration some pause.

Vietnam has enormously increased the people's distrust of the military. They no longer take what the military says on faith. How could they, after the last four or five years?

Two aspects of the ABM can be the focal points of public

discussion. One is that it will not increase our national security. It may endanger it. I don't think you can argue that with most people on a technical level, but you can say, "Here are the people who say it, and here are the ones on the other side." The question becomes the credibility of the defense establishment against the credibility of a large and distinguished group of outside experts and scholars.

I think we have a good chance when the people exercise that kind of judgment. In the primary elections in which I participated in 1968, people were willing to believe a judgment other than that of the defense establishment, even on military matters.

Secondly, and directly related to this, people now are much more worried about domestic problems than they were four or five years ago. Expenditures on ABM mean no increase of police in the streets, no chance of lowering property taxes, and an improved educational program deferred.

Dr. Barnet: We must come to see the problem of the military as an institutional and structural problem. The ABM provides a good illustration. It is a piece of technology in constant search for rationale, as General Ford pointed out. It shows there are forces which are not readily responsive either to public pressure or to rational analysis.

I don't think that is unusual or surprising or sinister in a conspiratorial sense. It represents the fact that we have built certain institutions that reinforce each other and close out other countervailing institutions. Unless we tackle this as an institutional problem, we will not really succeed—even if we win on the ABM, because these forces would move back with another weapon or perhaps with the ABM in a new, slightly revised form. Unless we begin to make a rather basic structural analysis and act on it in concrete ways, the most frightening images of the military-industrial complex will certainly become a reality in time.

On the other hand, we must not scare ourselves with the notion that this is all so big that there is nothing we can do.

IV

The Military Budget

We have been relying on the "new economics"—with its emphasis on using the federal budget to maintain economic stability and prevent cyclic depressions—without also recognizing that not all federal expenditures are of equal value to the nation. By placing the largest portion of our budget in the defense sector we have deeply disturbed the balance which societies must maintain between the civilian and military sectors of their governments and between their public and private outlays.

In our mistaken application of Keynesian economics we have failed to recognize that the nature of our public expenditures will determine the kind of society we build with the resulting economic growth. Some expenditures better society and enhance the quality of life for all our citizens while others, although they may seem to contribute to economic growth, in fact detract from our national well-being. We need to have a more accurate accounting of our economic growth, recognizing that some expenditures subtract from the nation's welfare even as they add to its economy.

In today's accounting both the production of cigarettes and expenditures on cancer research are counted as additions to economic growth; in fact, of course, they cancel each other out or, as at present, subtract from the health of our society. If we go ahead with the ABM and MIRV programs they will appear in our accounting as economic growth when in fact they will be destructive to the society, demanding further wasteful expenditures and making inevitable further decay in our cities and alienation of many of our people.

One must then ask whether our massive defense expenditure is in fact a way of dealing with foreign problems or whether it has become instead a way of preserving a pattern of advantage within the United States. The swollen military budget gives us, as individuals and as a society, a ready-made excuse to avoid facing our failure to achieve justice and equality for all our citizens.

The continuously increasing budget of the defense establishment offers vivid testimony that neither the executive nor the legislative branch is exercising proper control over our military programs and commitments. Defense expenditures rose from thirteen billion dollars in 1950 to forty-three billion in 1960 to more than eighty billion in 1969. There is every indication that they will continue to rise unless a major change in national priorities and budget practices is effected.

Conventional budget computations give only a partial picture of the immense impact of defense expenditures on the federal budget. In fiscal 1969, for instance, the sum for defense and defense-related outlays should be calculated to include 79.8 billion dollars for the Defense Department, military assistance programs, and atomic energy funds; 4.6 billion for space efforts; 7.1 billion for veterans' benefits, and 15.2 billion for interest on the national debt incurred in connection with military costs—a total of 106.7 billion dollars. All federal expenditures in the same fiscal year, excluding trust funds, totaled 136.3 billion dollars, of which defense and defense-related outlays constituted 78.5 per cent.

In fiscal 1970 the armed services' budget requests to the Secretary of Defense totaled one hundred ten billion dollars; these were reduced to eighty billion dollars in the Office of the Secretary of Defense. When the Vietnam war ends, the military will mount strenuous pressures to "catch up" on the items that have been deferred, including a large number of new ships, a new strategic missile, a new manned bomber, a battle tank, an antisubmarine aircraft, an Air Force interceptor, and a variety of other new weapons for an already bloated arsenal. Programs now approved will generate pressures for expansion as well. For instance, not only may the Army-developed Safeguard ABM system be augmented with additional radar sites and interceptor missiles, but the Navy is advocating development of its SABMIS system, a ship-based anti-ballistic missile system estimated to cost at least six billion dollars, and the Air Force is working on an airborne missile defense system to cost about sixteen billion dollars. Unless military spending is limited as a deliberate decision of national policy, the momentum of these institutions will carry the budget upward to ever higher levels.

A cessation of hostilities in Vietnam and a withdrawal of troops would make available about twenty billion dollars which could be allocated to domestic programs or other purposes. Considering only the present costs of approved systems and such fixed items as pay increases for military and civilian employees of the Pentagon, Charles Schultze estimates that the fiscal 1971 military budget for non-Vietnam purposes will be twelve to thirteen billion dollars higher than the current budget. By fiscal 1973 or 1974 the military budget will rise by twenty to twenty-five billion dollars on the basis of approved programs and pay increases alone.

This process of absorbing Vietnam savings in other parts of the military budget has already begun. The fiscal 1970 budget submitted by the Johnson Administration included a reduction of 3.5 billion dollars in the estimated costs of the Vietnam war. But this first installment in the "Vietnam dividend" was more than offset by an increase of more than six billion dollars in non-Vietnam military spending. Thus the first opportunity to transfer our Vietnam spending to civilian programs was passed up.

In the absence of any change in our defense plans the non-Vietnam military budget will increase by an amount sufficient to replace what we are spending in Vietnam. Indeed, there are reasons for thinking that actual spending will rise even higher. First, there will be an inevitable cost escalation as systems that have already been approved go into production, at a total cost of at least 3.6 billion dollars for fiscal 1970 alone. The costs of these systems are certain to rise. During the past fifteen years the average cost of a missile was three times the original estimate, while the cost of aircraft averaged a little more than twice the amount that had been expected. Recent experience with the F-111 fighter-bomber and the C-5A cargo plane shows that these "unexpected" rises are still normal.

Second, the new weapons proposed by the armed services but not yet approved by the Secretary of Defense will cost large sums of money if they are accepted in succeeding years. Further, if we go ahead with ABM and MIRV there will be an escalation in the cost of our strategic forces as the Soviet Union reacts to these weapons and we respond to their reactions.

The American economy will continue to grow even without significant inflation, generating fifteen to seventeen billion dollars a year more in federal revenues. Five years from now the total growth—or "fiscal" dividend—will provide one hundred billion dollars in federal funds above those being spent today. However, the various claims on this dividend, including those from the military, will make this gain illusory, at least under present circumstances.

If we assume that the income-tax surcharge will be dropped once the Vietnam war is over and that existing federal programs will increase in cost even without program improvement simply to take account of a growing population, then the one-hundred-billion-dollar fiscal dividend by fiscal 1974 will be reduced to about thirty billion dollars. The increase in weapons system costs described above could easily consume the thirty billion, leaving nothing for new or expanded domestic programs. This estimate assumes unchanged tax rates except for the dropped surcharge. Clearly, as Charles Schultze says, a United States which every five years adds to its productive output the equivalent of the output of West Germany can do anything it sets its mind to with that growth, including transferring a large portion of it to public uses rather than private consumption. Now as a practical political matter it seems unlikely that existing tax rates will be raised very much.

So, if domestic programs must have substantially more funds, these must come from the bloated budget of the Defense Department.

Robert Benson, a former Defense Department official, has suggested that even without any change in our foreign policy or military objectives, the Pentagon could save at least nine billion dollars by eliminating duplicatory programs, by reducing inefficient turnover in the assignment of military officers and effecting other efficiencies in the use of military manpower, by changing contracting practices so that greater performance and economy are required of the contractors, by eliminating unneeded and obsolete weapons systems, and by cutting back some of our unnecessary overseas troop deployment. A careful and critical examination of the military budget, reviewing the purposes of our armed forces in relation to our foreign-policy goals as well as the effect of the defense establishment on the country, could result in substantial added savings. But Congress must develop the will and the structure to do this.

Present force levels assume that the United States must be prepared to fight three wars simultaneously: a nuclear war originating in Europe, a major conventional war in the China area, and a small war elsewhere in the third world (for instance, in Latin America). Assuming this, almost any force level can be justified. Substantial reductions can be made if more realistic contingencies are assumed and the defense of our own shores is taken as the primary and proper role of our armed forces.

Our armed forces could be cut down by at least a million men. Reductions in the cost of maintaining ready forces, as well as savings from a halt in our strategic arms buildup— and, of course, a halt in the Vietnam conflict—could reduce defense expenditures by more than fifty billion dollars to pre-1960 levels.

Professor Boulding: The military budget is a function of our own image of ourselves as a nation and of our image of the international environment. That is, it is a function of our desire for power and our sense of being threatened. Of these, the first is considerably under our control, and the second may be controlled in part by a shift in policy. One thing we must learn is that the national interest is a variable and not a constant. The national interest is what the nation is interested in. Within wide limits, this is a subjective variable. If we have an image of ourselves as *the* great power, making everyone else conform to our wishes, we will tend to have a large war industry. If we visualize ourselves playing a more modest role in the international system, albeit perhaps as first among equals, we can get along with a much smaller war industry.

From a strictly economic point of view, being a great power is extremely unrewarding. The Swedes discovered this a hundred years ago, the British and the French have just discovered it in this generation, but we do not yet understand it. There is little doubt that the economic development of Britain and France, for instance, was seriously hampered by their imperial and great-power positions in the hundred years after 1850. The development of the United States in this period was unquestionably assisted by the fact that it did not visualize itself as a great power and hence devoted a very small proportion of its resources to the war industry. In the next generation or so, if we persist in our image of ourselves as not only a great power but the greatest power, we shall not only greatly increase the risk of mutual destruction but seriously hamper our nation's development and the quality of our national life.

External threats are not unreal, but they tend to loom larger in the popular imagination than they really are. Furthermore, our own almost exclusive reliance on the threat system in our international relations increases rather than decreases the external threat. Our foreign relations now are fantastically unbalanced on the side of threat. We may visualize our armed forces merely as counterthreat, but the rest of the world does not see it in these terms. We need to have a more balanced foreign policy which would be quite consciously directed to the establishment of stable peace and which would place greater stress on the development of integrative and trade relationships rather than on the use of threat.

The American eagle is portrayed as holding an olive branch in one claw and a sheaf of arrows in the other. What kind of policy is it that weighs down one claw with eighty billion dollars' worth of arrows and provides the other with a minute, wilted olive branch costing practically nothing?

Whatever may have been true in the past, in the modern world the main economic damage done by any military organization is to its own nation. Thus the U.S. Department of Defense does a great deal of economic damage to the United States: it reduces domestic consumption by about fifteen per cent, and, by diverting the growth resource into the rat hole of competitive weapons systems, or even space technology, it diminishes the annual rate of economic growth, probably by as much as two per cent. This means that the cost of the military establishment is much more than the nine or ten per cent of the gross national product it occupies.

We have now reached the point where even during a war the economic damage done to a country by its own military is apt to be greater than the damage it inflicts on the enemy. Thus in 1944 the Japanese military withdrew some forty-five per cent of the Japanese GNP, and it is doubtful whether all the destruction wreaked by the U.S. Air Force amounted to as much as that. In the United States this phenomenon was masked by the fact that the expansion of the military forces in World War II came largely out of unemployed persons, but even so the economic damage done by our own military far exceeded the damage caused by our enemies.

The economic costs of the military become even more apparent when we reflect that these costs come not merely out of the economy at large but out of what I call the "grants economy"—that is, the part of the economic system in which resources are allocated and distributed mainly by one-way transfers rather than by exchange. Thus the grants economy includes most of the government tax and expenditure system outside of what might be called "government business" such as the post office, and it also includes the greater part of private charitable grants and foundation grants. The grants sector is an "economy" in the sense that the total of grants is not indefinitely expansible but depends on the society's general willingness to make one-way transfers. The size of the grants economy varies from country to country, but it is seldom more than twenty per cent of the gross national product; even in socialist societies a very large part of the economy is still governed by exchange. The total size of the grants economy is a function of the strength of the sense of community in the area within which the grants are being made.

From the individual's point of view, a very large proportion of the tax system is in the grants economy, in the sense that he does not get anything tangible and specific for his taxes. A democratic society can easily run into tax resistance if the people feel that the grants economy has grown beyond what their sense of community will support. We see this, for instance, in the frequent failure of voters to approve school bonds and millage increases, and we see it in political resistance to increased federal taxes. At any one moment it is clear that the total of the grants economy cannot be expanded very much except through a change in the system, such as occurs during war, which greatly increases the sense of community.

If the grants economy is an "economy," however, it is subject to the law of scarcity; that is, if I get a grant, somebody else doesn't. The person who does not get a grant is usually not aware of who benefits from his loss. The whole structure of alternative costs in the grants economy is much less visible than it is in the exchange economy. This ignorance in the absence of feedback makes decisions in the grants economy easier but also makes them more subject to error. To use an old but still serviceable piece of rhetoric, when the

Ford Motor Company produces an Edsel it soon finds out, because one of the virtues in the exchange system is very rapid feedback. When the Department of Defense produces an Edsel it may not find out for twenty years. And when the Ford Foundation produces an Edsel it probably never finds out. There is, however, growing awareness of the alternative cost structure of the grants economy, and this is likely to produce increasingly potent coalitions against the military.

The war industry is now more than half the grants sector of the economy, so it is clear that it bites much more severely into this sector than it does into the economy as a whole. Thus the segments of the economy most affected by the war industry are those which are competitive with it in the structure of one-way transfers. The question, "Who loses a dollar when the military gains one?" is a very legitimate question, even though the fact that the grants economy is not completely rigid means that when the military gains a dollar someone else may lose only ninety cents. Although the answer to this question may vary from time to time, it seems clear from the evidence of the last thirty years that the principal victim of an expansion of the military budget is the education industry, though other civilian sectors of the grants economy also suffer.

The effect on education is likely to be an increasingly serious problem simply because education as an industry and as a proportion of the gross national product must expand very rapidly in the coming years. There are two reasons for this. One is that as the total stock of knowledge increases the resources that have to be put into transmitting it to the next generation likewise must increase. The second reason is that as the productivity of education rises slowly, if at all, the relative price of education continually rises—in the form of rising wages and salaries for those engaged in it, who must get their share of the increasing per-capita product of the society. Education, however, is mainly financed through the grants economy, especially through the tax system, and it is even now running into severe resistance to expansion, as evidenced in the failure of school bonds and millage increases, and the failure of central-city school systems to cope with the flood of rural migrants. Even though the decline in the birth rate is likely to make this problem somewhat easier in the future, the increase in the burden of transmitting knowledge will accelerate rather than slow down.

The war industry may be costly to future generations in another respect: in its absorption of a very large proportion (some have estimated sixty per cent) of research-and-development expenditures. There is much evidence to suggest that civilian industry is deprived of able research scientists and engineers because of the "internal brain drain" into the war industry. By far the most important resource for any society's *future* is the innovative capacity of its ablest minds. If these are absorbed into the war industry they will clearly not be available elsewhere. Furthermore, the spill-overs from the war industry into the civilian sector seem to have been declining and are quite inadequate to compensate for the drain. Because of the obsessive expansion of the war industry, many vital sectors of the civilian economy are failing to solve their technical problems. We see this in transportation, in building, even in many areas of general manufacturing. Ship-building is a case where the domination of an industry by the war industry has resulted in technical backwardness because even within the war industry itself certain areas, such as the aerospace complex, have absorbed problem-solving capacity at the expense of others.

The war industry is a cancer within the body of American society. It has its own mode of growth, it represents a system which is virtually independent and indeed objectively inimical to the welfare of the American people, in spite of the fact that it visualizes itself as their protector. We have not yet lost civilian control over the war industry, but if this control is not reasserted we are in grave danger of going the way of

Japan—a country conquered by its own war industry in the middle 1930s, with eventually catastrophic consequences.

Professor Schultze: Let me summarize one aspect of the cost of maintaining our present and projected national security institutions—that is, the budgetary cost—and relate that to what might be available for domestic programs.

An economy like ours, which continues to grow even without significant inflation, will generate something like fifteen to seventeen billion dollars in additional revenues each year. We might look forward to a cessation of hostilities in Vietnam and the withdrawal of U.S. troops: there is another twenty billion dollars in budgetary savings which, one might think, would be available for domestic programs of one kind or another—for funding additional federal programs, or funding existing programs adequately, or revenue sharing with the states, tax cuts, and the like.

You would think, if you looked at it this way, that five years from now you would have one hundred billion dollars—five times sixteen plus twenty—as a fiscal dividend that we could use for these domestic purposes.

However, if you begin to look at the various claims on this dividend, including the military claims, it turns out that under present circumstances this is clearly illusory. Let me list three things on the military side likely to chew heavily into that hundred-billion-dollar figure.

First, weapons systems already approved. These are all familiar to you—Minuteman III, Poseidon, the Safeguard ABM, four nuclear-powered aircraft carriers, forty new destroyers, a new class of fast-attack submarines, a new Navy fighter interceptor. All of these have been approved and are in the works. If you look at their present costs and take into account such things as pay increases for military and civilian employes, it is my own rough estimate that the fiscal 1971 defense budget for non-Vietnam purposes will be twelve to thirteen billion dollars higher than the current budget.

It has not been generally noticed that the fiscal 1970 defense budget for non-Vietnam purposes submitted by President Johnson and modified by Secretary Laird was already six to six and a half billion dollars higher than that for fiscal 1969. Already you have a six-billion-dollar down payment in the budget on these items.

The total defense budget itself in fiscal 1970 was unchanged from 1969, but Vietnam was projected down by three and a half billion and non-Vietnam was projected up by four billion dollars. To that you add another two and a half billion dollars as the cost of military and civilian pay increases. Finally, subtract the half-billion-dollar cut which was made in non-Vietnam spending. This leaves a six-billion-dollar increase in effect in the non-Vietnam military budget in fiscal 1970 alone.

We can thus project increases over 1969 of twelve to thirteen billion dollars by 1971, and probably twenty to twenty-five billion dollars by fiscal 1973 or 1974, just on the basis of already approved programs plus pay increases and price increases. Therefore there is a high probability that the non-Vietnam budget will by fiscal 1973 or 1974 have risen by an amount sufficient to replace what we are spending in Vietnam. Even if peace is achieved in Vietnam and the United States withdraws, the defense budget will by unchanged.

Let me add three other factors which have to be taken into account, possibly making my estimates too conservative.

First, cost escalation. Studies show that during the 1950s and early 1960s the average actual unit cost of missiles produced was three times the original estimated cost. For fighter aircraft the ratio was something like 2.2 or 2.3. Or take the Sentinel ABM: originally announced at 4.4 billion dollars, the cost had risen in a year to 5.5 billion. The latest number kicking around unpublished before Sentinel was changed to Safeguard was 9.5 billion dollars. I think that is fairly typical. The first nuclear aircraft carrier was estimated at 430 million dollars. Late in 1967 the estimate was raised to 540 million dollars. I don't know what it is now but I am sure it is at least 600 million dollars.

The projections I have given assume the *presently* estimated costs. Undoubtedly they will eventually be higher, but I have not calculated that into my figures.

Second, I have not counted in new weapons systems proposed but not yet approved: a new advanced strategic bomber —whose ten-year systems cost would probably be twelve billion dollars; a new strategic missile in superhard silos; a new strategic defense interceptor aircraft; a new main battle tank; a Navy antisubmarine plane; and a new Air Force air-to-air combat aircraft. These are all high on the Joint Chiefs' list of priorities.

Third, none of the categories I have discussed allows for the dynamics of escalation between the Soviets and us with respect to nuclear forces. I have not included in these projections an allowance for the second-round effects of going ahead with MIRV and Safeguard.

The sum and substance of all this is that by simply maintaining our presently approved military posture—with no major cost escalation, with no new weapons systems of any significant kind approved—current spending plans will roughly match the Vietnam dividend by about fiscal 1974, give or take three or four billion dollars. Only a former Budget Director could blithely say "give or take three or four billion dollars," but in terms of the magnitudes we are talking about it is well within the limits of good estimation.

Therefore, if I finally take into account the other claims on that fiscal dividend—including a cut in the tax surcharge or elimination of it, plus the inevitability of increases in existing civilian programs simply on account of a growing population and other "built-in" costs—my estimates take that potential one hundred billion dollars available for social uses five years from now and reduce it by fiscal 1974 to about thirty billion dollars on my *conservative* assumptions about military spending. Looking at some of the real possibilities for arms escalation, this thirty billion dollars could be further sharply reduced.

I don't need to spell out that in many important areas the only way we can solve our social problems is through relatively sizable expenditures. I do not happen to believe that money alone will solve the problems, but it will be a necessary condition in many areas. To do anything really significant, you cannot do it cheaply. To give two examples, I cannot conceive of a decent income-maintenance program being done on the cheap—one you try to do that way may do more harm than good—nor can I conceive of doing much about compensatory education on the cheap.

I assumed in all these calculations unchanged tax rates except for the dropped surcharge. Clearly, from the point of view of logic and economics, a United States which every five years adds to its productivity base the equivalent of a West German economy can do anything it sets its mind to with that growth. But as a practical political matter we are not about to do anything radically different from what we are doing now.

I think you might as well resign yourself to looking within the existing tax rates, roughly, for the funds available for an attack on major social problems. This is not logically or economically necessary, but I think it is politically realistic.

Mr. Goodwin: Much of the problem we are discussing has a more recent origin than some of the comments suggest.

Two of the villains, I think, are the Harvard University Department of Economics and the Harvard Business School: one for having introduced the "new economics," which persuaded the U.S. Government that it was all right to spend enormous amounts of money—money for which the military became a natural outlet; and the other for introducing management techniques into the Pentagon that made the military far more efficient in pursuit of their requests than they ever were before. It has given them the whole rubric of strategic theory which enables them to justify a request for almost any weapons system. And it has reduced the classic rivalry among the services, which in the past allowed a President to balance off one service against the other. Under President Eisenhower generals were resigning in protest and the military budget was half what it is now. Under President Truman, until Korea, the military was slashed almost to nothing. We are talking about a phenomenon of the 1960s and the machine that was built between 1960 and now.

Because this power, this technological apparatus, has been given to the Defense Department, I doubt if it is possible ever to win arguments decisively on individual weapons systems. There is no limit to the ingenuity by which they can justify particular weapons systems or a particular base or a particular program. There is almost no limit, no theoretical limit, to what can be justified as in some way or another increasing our security.

What we have to do, therefore, is go back almost to where we were about 1960 and say there are some risks that we won't accept and some that we will. One risk we will not accept—to the extent that we can prevent it—is the risk of being blown up by the Russians. That is obviously unacceptable, so nuclear deterrence is a critical element. Beyond that, there are few world situations that could arise where we would not have adequate time to build from the large reserves we have, from our tremendous productive capacity, to meet danger if it arises.

The notion that we must maintain a constantly accelerated level of technological development, new weapons, armies just to sit around or cruise the seven seas waiting for something to happen—this notion makes no sense to me. I can't think of a situation where we have not had adequate time to respond. Had we had a much smaller standing army, we still would have had time in Vietnam to call up the reserves and build to our present level in the same period of time available. In Korea we had a small army and were able to build from reserves.

Maybe what I'm suggesting is almost a return to the doctrine of massive retaliation as a military strategy. I don't think there is any hope of cutting severely into the military budget when the debate shifts to terminology, a debate which only the military can win.

Senator Saxbe: I think Mr. Goodwin has hit on a very important point. We don't dare be drawn off into the thicket of individual problems in military affairs because once we are there, there is no stopping. We don't have to meet this issue here, this point there. We should concentrate on the assumption of risk: the risk of peace. We must turn the focus from the risk of war to the gamble for peace. We can't say that we shall guarantee in every instance that there will not be a disruption here or there in the world. But getting away from the fear that Dr. Galbraith spoke about would be a breath of fresh air, not only for this country but for the world.

V

Congress—the Need for Leadership

The Congress of the United States has failed to exercise its Constitutional function of supervising the raising of our armed forces and overseeing their use in foreign wars. Instead, a vast national security apparatus has been created with the silent acquiescence of Congress.

Tens of billions of dollars are appropriated for the Defense Department with little or no debate, and the views of the public are seldom sought. In one series of hearings before the House Armed Services Committee, covering three thousand pages of testimony, three hundred witnesses appeared; 298 came from the Defense Department and two from the National Rifle Association. With this imbalance in perspective, it is not surprising that there has been only the most superficial examination of defense expenditures.

Congress must challenge the military assumptions and programs of the executive branch and assume responsibility for the future military affairs of this country. To do this it must have not only new institutions that permit it to gather the information and insights it needs, but a new view of itself and its function in American society.

Since the defense budget sets the direction of our economy and foreign policy for years to come, its size and content should be the subject of probing Congressional study and debate. At present, however, the budget receives only superficial attention from most Representatives and Senators. Congress does not have the capacity to make detailed comparisons of weapons systems and military programs, and even if it did, this would not provide the necessary resource material for the exercise of Congressional authority. Technical decisions on the design of weaponry are properly made by military officers and defense officials, but the desirability of individual weapons systems cannot be assessed without examining the foreign-policy objectives they are supposed to serve. With respect to ABM and MIRV, for example, the questions that must be raised center on whether we are prepared to accept a situation of mutual deterrence and relative parity with the Soviet Union or whether we should continue to seek an offensive first-strike capability. Similarly, the issues raised by our overseas bases go far deeper than the desirability of air conditioning in the officers' quarters—the type of problem that has occupied a considerable portion of the time of the Armed Services Committees.

Many members of Congress feel an urgent need for more facts in dealing effectively with the military. With greater information they could question more competently and persuasively the funding requests for weapons and standing forces. But additional information alone will make it no easier for Congress to control the military—as witness the performance of the Armed Services Committees, which are deluged with technical data and evaluations but, having failed to develop an independent basis for judging relative priorities, they have been unable to make effective use of their surfeit of information. It is not classified facts which Congress needs, but a world view which can challenge the military's analysis. The analytical methods increasingly relied on by the executive branch tend to focus attention on technical means, with policy ends lost in a maze of figures and charts. Congress must develop its own perspective, using an independent set of operating assumptions.

The United States maintains military installations around the world, including 429 major and 2972 minor overseas military bases staffed by a million men. These cost us billions of dollars, disturb our international balance of payments, and create implicit commitments which return to haunt us when crises erupt. Yet most of these bases are maintained simply because they were set up long ago—not because a public evaluation of our national objectives indicates they are needed now.

Congress should be asking why such bases were established and what national commitments are involved in their retention. Such basic decisions are now made by the executive branch in a context that minimizes debate, avoids critical consideration of costs as well as benefits, and often does not even bring before Congress or the American people the fundamental decisions when they are made.

There is no lack of examples of Congressional default. We are currently going into procurement of the F-14 aircraft for the Navy and Marine forces. Over the ten-year period in which that aircraft will be operational, the total cost of the program will be at least twenty billion dollars. But Congress has never adequately examined the contingencies and military assumptions on which this new aircraft is based.

We spend ten to twelve billion dollars a year maintaining forces sufficient to fight China in a land war in Asia—the explicit assumption on which our military strength is founded, but which has never been subjected to national debate. In fact, most Americans are unaware of its existence as a factor in the formulation of the nation's military posture.

The Pentagon now provides the sole framework for any debate on military policy. No other national institution can perform the requisite analyses and provide an adequate counterweight to the Pentagon assessment. A major overhaul of the Congressional committee structure may be needed before such a counterinstitution can develop. The current committee structure evolved before the executive branch adopted the tools of technology and modern economic analysis. The committees tend to look for direction to the executive branch rather than to the country and its people, discovering our people's needs and consulting with them to find answers. The existing committee structure could work if Congress wished to take hold of the issue, recognize the need for fundamental questioning of the defense establishment, and re-establish its authority in military affairs. It could then confront the executive branch on how well it was meeting the needs of the country. The Senate Committee on Foreign Relations, in its examination of the ABM issue early in 1969, has shown that this can be done on a single, well-focused issue. In general, however, the rigid committee framework has prevented such boundary-crossing.

When the institutions exist for confronting the executive and particularly the military, they will be a focus for those private citizens and research institutes which now possess information that Congress could use. These groups now can offer their knowledge and insights only to individual Representatives and Senators who are concerned about particular issues. New Congressional institutions would provide a continuing base for gathering such information and developing a perspective permitting its effective use.

An effective dialogue must be restored within this country on our foreign and military policies. New mechanisms must be created within Congress to provide institutional support to sustain this dialogue. The present structure tends to compartmentalize decisions, and it must be surmounted.

Congress can successfully challenge the military establishment only if it develops an authoritative perspective for questioning the judgment of the Defense Department. The decisive questions of national security are not scientific or managerial but moral and political—and on such questions the people and the people's representatives are as qualified to pass judgment as the so-called experts. Even if they do not know the technical intricacies of a piece of military hardware, they can assess the likely consequences of the use of that hardware. And they will not be burdened with the pressures felt within the bureaucracy to produce any new weapon just because it can be built.

Modern techniques of systems analysis have allowed the Pentagon to support a request for almost any weapons system and have curtailed the interservice rivalry that formerly allowed the President to restrain such requests by balancing one service against another. Congress therefore finds it difficult to win decisively on an individual program, but general policies and national priorities should be set, and requests for individual items should be required to conform to these guidelines.

For Congress to escape from the present bureaucratic trap, it must have new ways of considering the budget. It should begin by holding budget hearings in Congressional districts and in the states, asking the American people how they want their money spent, whether they want to continue spending the largest portion of their tax dollar on the Vietnam war and future wars. Grass-roots hearings in each of the Congressional districts around the country would provide a forum for exposing social conditions. They could serve to mobilize the public to insist that tax dollars be spent on the real needs of the people of our nation.

These hearings could take place each fall and winter. Then, rather than passively receiving the President's State of the Union message and waiting for his program, Congress could engage in extended debate early in the spring, conducting its own State of the Nation examination, developing its own perspective on priorities for the nation, on the basis of which it would provide directives to the various committees that apportion the federal budget among the agencies of the executive branch.

Congress could develop a new kind of national budget, divided not along agency lines but apportioned according to national needs. It could insist that the executive branch—particularly the Defense Department—present its budget requests in terms of objectives or "missions," rather than in a framework of "forces-in-being." It could ask how well our military programs serve the foreign-policy objectives of the United States, rather than how sophisticated is the hardware we are buying. It could ask how well we are doing as a nation in educating our populace, providing for its health needs, and protecting its environment.

In this way Congress would place the military budget in a setting where it would be compared with other national programs, providing the transfer mechanism present lacking in the budget process. Another advantage of such a broad look would be a clearer understanding of how specific federal programs affect each locality. If a particular defense program were cut back, Congress could see which areas of the country would be affected and what other federal programs might be increased to minimize economic dislocations. Congress would thus open to public discussion the entire question of the federal role in facilitating conversions from one set of priorities to another.

Congress will also have to deal more directly with the problem of military secrecy. The security classification system must be drastically revised. Much less information must be kept behind bars. Decisions reached today behind closed doors in the executive branch must be brought before Congress, together with all the relevant facts, for its over-all policy judgment.

Congress should take a fresh look at why information is classified. From whom is the information meant to be kept? (The Soviet government clearly knows far more about our military operations than the American public does.) Just whom is the classification system protecting? Can we do away with the system altogether? It is, after all, a relatively new institution in American life, yet it plays a major role in protecting the national security apparatus from public criticism and control. Congress should insist on its right to know what the defense establishment is doing. It has allowed the Pentagon full discretion in using security classifications, forgetting that we diminish our freedom each time an additional matter of national policy is kept from the public.

To cite one example of the misuse of classification, the MIRV program was developed and carried on for three years without the knowledge of most members of Congress. While the Armed Services Committees were informed, they did not appear to question the value or desirability of the program; the rest of Congress was not informed of it. Only through press leaks long after the program had begun did the public become aware of its existence, and its full significance became apparent much later still.

While in principle the absence of detailed information

need not prevent Congress from exercising its proper function of oversight, in practice no Congressman feels equipped to cope with defense problems unless he is buttressed with full and authoritative information. The Congressman must have an answer to the assertion often made by those "in the know" that "if you only knew what I know, you wouldn't feel this way." Rational arguments can be a partial answer to this, but only authoritative information can remove the uncertainty which such an approach creates.

Advice is often sought from outside individuals who are believed to have security clearance and access to defense information. However, except on narrow issues of military technology, almost no presently classified information cannot be obtained as well from a careful reading of the newspapers. Thus, an absence of classified information need not prevent Congressmen from making the policy judgments they should be making.

In particular, more timely information must be available to Congress to enable its members to end the practice of voting funds for programs about which they know nothing. Congress should insist that the executive branch take the risk involved in releasing classified information, rather than erode the democratic process by having decisions on the allocation of national resources made on the basis of secret information. Greater disclosure might even improve the information available to the executive branch, since classified information is sometimes proved wrong (e.g., many past projections on the course of the Vietnam war) but is not subject to debate and challenge because of its classification.

Congress and the public need the assistance of many experts and independent research centers who can bring the informed analyses of the academic community to bear on our defense budget and foreign policy. These should be funded by private foundations so that their views of government programs are both independent and various. They need not have access to classified information and, indeed, might benefit from not having this restraint on their ability to criticize the defense establishment.

But they alone cannot provide the full resources Congress

needs for a successful confrontation with the military. There should also be a permanent Defense Review Office, analogous to the General Accounting Office, providing Congress with independent reviews of Defense Department programs. This agency would have access to top-secret information and would be as fully informed as the advocates of weapons programs within the Defense Department. It could, for instance, alert Congress to programs like the MIRV project and the extensive chemical and biological warfare program maintained by the armed services, which many members have only recently discovered. A Defense Review Office would also provide a group of independent, well-informed civilians working full-time to examine the desirability of particular budgetary decisions. It might also have associated with it a senior consulting board as an advisory arm to Congress, available for informed judgment as one equalizer to the present disparity in expertise between Congress and the executive branch.

Unfortunately, past experience with non-Congressional bodies does not provide much hope that over a long period they can remain truly independent and capable of providing fundamental criticism of Defense Department programs. It is, indeed, questionable whether any group could maintain the necessary independence over the long run except a group of Congressmen, since only Congressmen would have the necessary Constitutional authority or political base support to demand answers to critical questions from the executive branch.

There are organs in Congress now which have access to information and independent political power, and they should undertake this type of analysis and criticism. There is no reason why the Armed Services Committees must spend their time examining the minutiae of military programs. Under their present leadership, though, these committees cannot be depended on to provide useful examinations of broad policy issues. The Congress therefore must turn to some other mechanism.

An instrument to overcome the rigidities of the present structure could be based on the precedent of the Temporary National Economic Committee which functioned in the late

1930s. Congress could establish a Temporary National Security Committee composed of members of Congress and qualified outside experts. The original TNEC conducted a searching study of the structure of the American economy— one that is still an outstanding source on the national economy before World War II. A Temporary National Security Committee could look at the institutional structure of the military-industrial complex, the relation between military policy and the economic interests which depend on the military establishment, and the economic and social impact of this enterprise upon American society.

Congress could also create a Joint Committee on National Priorities along the lines of the Joint Economic Committee set up after World War II, to conduct continuing, broad investigations into the implications and objectives of American defense policy and its relative priority in the national budget. The Secretary of State could be asked to deliver a "posture statement" to Congress in much the same manner as the Secretary of Defense does now, defining the assumptions and objectives of our foreign policy. These statements could be reviewed and analyzed by this joint committee, providing a focus for the annual Congressional debate on national issues.

Any new Congressional institutions alone cannot accomplish the task. Congress as a whole must act more meaningfully, with each member dealing with a much broader field than customarily falls within the domain of an individual committee. The members of Congress must be more effective representatives of the people on broad issues of national policy, rather than simply experts on narrow subjects, making policy for the entire nation in their committees. Congress could then redress the balance of power which is today so skewed in favor of the executive branch.

More thorough review of national programs by Congress could generate more careful examination of them in the executive branch as well. The existence of a Joint Committee on National Priorities would, for instance, encourage the Bureau of the Budget to probe more deeply into military policy than it has in the past. Congress should also, through the Government Operations Committee or another appropriate body, begin on its own initiative to propose machinery whereby real issues of "social cost effectiveness" could be raised within the executive branch, particularly where military needs could be compared with nonmilitary requirements. Perhaps the cabinet must evolve into an operating agency with the authority to examine issues of national priorities so as not to leave the military budget "above the battle" as it is now.

One possible way of dealing with the current power relationships, and altering them over a period of time, would be to apply a steadily decreasing dollar limitation to the military budget—of just what degree to be determined from a reassessment of national priorities within Congress—forcing defense officials to limit their operations and cut back the far-flung expanse of the armed forces. Just as there is no end to the possible weapons that can be sought, and no absolute criterion for deciding whether to purchase them, so there is no authoritative scientific standard which can be used to decide the amount by which the budget should be reduced each year. This is more a political than a technical issue, depending upon Congress' assessment of the place of American military force in the world and the rapidity with which it would like to see a transition to an economy geared more to our domestic needs.

Representative Rosenthal: Concern and indignation have brought us together. The country is growing impatient about the size of the defense budget and its social effects.

We, the Congressional sponsors of this discussion, are alarmed about this situation and share this deep concern with our constituents. But we believe that Congress as a whole has not shown sufficient sensitivity to these issues and to the public's anxieties about them. We must accelerate awareness of the dangers in the defense budget, the arms race, and the militarization of our society.

As committed public officials and representatives of a troubled people, our concerns are:

A country which continues to wage war when that war is discredited;

The missiles and anti-missiles which proliferate—while citizens wonder what else this generation of defense experts has in store;

The hundred billion dollars allotted for defense in a single year, when Teacher Corps funds are reduced by half;

The two-thirds of all tax receipts that are spent for defense —more than all federal, state, and local outlays for social security, health, education, housing, and agriculture;

A military budget which rises each year, spurred by a seemingly self-generating mechanism, functioning with little or no attention to merit.

The magnitude and urgency of these problems are obvious. The answers are less obvious. But the search for answers must continue this year and throughout the years to come, as long as we are threatened by our own machinery of war.

Dr. Larson: We are at a turning point now in our whole military policy. It is long overdue for a complete reappraisal and overhaul.

Think of some of the changes of the past few years. For one, we have learned, without any doubt at all, that we can't have everything we want on the military side and have everything we need on the domestic side. We used to hear speeches about how we could have them both. We now know better. This transforms the whole discussion of the military budget: Instead of starting out to see how much the military establishment needs and dividing up what is left over for everybody else, we are heading into a period when we will have an honest competition among the demands of our domestic economy—education programs, industry programs, and the rest.

In the past we seemed sometimes to have a contest—I sat in on some of those budget discussions in the Cabinet—but it was never a fair fight. The outcome was judged in advance.

We would hear that "our boys overseas must have anything they need." Now people are beginning to say, "Our children back home must have things they need, too."

Second, we have learned that we can't be the world's policeman. Everybody says that nowadays, though few were saying it a few years ago. Then we were saying, "If there is a threat to freedom anywhere at any time, we will be there." Few talk like that any more.

The third big change is that we now have to approach our military budget as a part of the total political environment—part of the question of what kind of world this is and what role we will play in it.

Military policy must be a function of political policy, and not the other way around. Instead of permitting essentially political decisions to be governed by military considerations and commitments, we will have to decide in advance how we are going to use our strength. The world power situation has been profoundly changed since we adopted the basic military policies that we still seem to be following.

It is not overstating the case, for example, to say that the Soviet Union and the People's Republic of China are at war with each other today. This has transformed the world from what it was when people assumed there was only one real contest—the contest between the Soviet Union and the United States—and when an anti-Soviet stance was the beginning and end of our policy. Our military decisions were based on the idea that the moment one power or the other obtained even a small nuclear superiority over the other it would obliterate its opponent. Let me suggest that we have a much different balance-of-power situation in the world today. Why would the Soviet Union want to obliterate the United States when it has a war on its hands with the Chinese? This is something to ponder. There are many other great changes.

Finally, there is a new feeling in Congress about its relations to foreign policy and its responsibilities. Many members of the Senate and the House feel they may not have done all they could have in the crucial period when Vietnam policy was being formed. They are determined to do something different from this point on.

Representative Leggett: I would hope that this discussion could orient itself toward setting a national policy on a reasonable relationship between defense expenditures and domestic expenditures.

If we could settle on that and settle that we would like to do this within the framework of a balanced budget, I think we might make a meaningful contribution toward our own security and domestic progress. We have to get into a balanced economy again. When we sanction continuous inflation, it seems to me it is nothing more than theft from people on fixed income—the poor, the old, and the retired.

I would not like to substitute my judgment for the judgment of General Powers or General Wheeler or some of the other experts in our defense structure. I would rather stand back and say, "Let's agree that a certain percentage of our income should be voted for defense—say fifty or sixty per cent of our federal budget."

Then you could apportion that among the various services and let them provide the best defense possible within that framework. Unless we do that, they have up their sleeve in the Department of Defense more than twenty billion dollars' worth of new systems, in addition to the ABM. There is going to be tremendous pressure to deploy those systems, and I think many are needed. But I would rather not have us decide on a political basis which of them to deploy. I would rather have the decision made by the professional soldiers we have trained with our tax dollars.

Mr. Goodwin: The problem of the military budget is not the problem of the Joint Chiefs of Staff, whose business it is to rely on force, but the problem of the civilian leadership of the Pentagon and the President of the United States. They have the ultimate power of decision.

In the past history of this country, many Presidents—

including the late President Eisenhower—have been willing to impose their will on the military. No one can expect generals to stop thinking like generals. If they did, they wouldn't be very useful.

One more point: I think there is a need for those who are informed to make information available about the military budget. There are people on the outside who have just about as much knowledge as anybody in the Pentagon and sometimes better judgment—often people who worked in past administrations. I have never found it difficult in a primary or Presidential campaign to get access to the best thinking available on this subject.

If the new politics means anything, it means that somehow this issue has to be made real in terms of the choices between education and missiles, the choices in housing, tax rates, and all the rest of it, and weapons systems. You could build up that kind of feeling in the country. The feeling is already there in response to the ABM; three years ago the idea of mass meetings anywhere in the country over an issue like the anti-ballistic missile system would have been incredible.

Any informed group can help by making itself available to Congress, making this issue its first priority, because public pressure is what makes it possible for Congress to act, and makes it more likely that Congress *will* act, as a restraining force. Congress alone against the President is helpless in the military field.

Professor Falk: If we were to establish some sensible priorities in the genuine security needs of the United States, we would find that a military budget of between ten and twenty-five per cent of the present level would be more than sufficient to deal with threats that confront the United States, and that establishing such a budget would have all kinds of beneficial side effects. It would, for example, make the military justify their priorities in a much more intelligent way. They have never been forced to operate within a fixed framework. I am really elaborating on what Representative Leggett said —that we need to establish a fixed ceiling, and then work on the priorities on that basis.

Dr. Barnet: I agree very much with what Representative Leggett and Dr. Falk have said. The momentum of military institutions will continually push the budget up unless military spending is limited by a deliberate decision at the highest level of national policy.

We could begin to look at specific elements of the military budget in terms of the rationale offered for them. If you look at the historical rationale for overseas bases, for example, the initial one was that they were needed because there were no intercontinental forces available in the U.S. Air Force. When it became clear that that was no longer the situation, the Air Force and Department of Defense came up with other rationalizations—political rationalizations—for keeping those bases, contending that the United States must have presence for political reasons in many of the countries where we had bases. This is a prime example of how the military have been allowed to determine the basic national interest of the United States. In none of these cases is it in our interest to have our primary relationship with another country defined by military presence. Both in military security terms and in terms of having better relations with those countries, we would be better served if the bases were gone.

Professor Galbraith: We must find means of taking advantage of the fact that the government no longer has a monopoly of scientific and inside knowledge. I wonder, for example, whether the time hasn't come to constitute some kind of civilian audit authority which would make use of the very large amount of talent that was at one time associated with the Pentagon and that isn't bemused by talk of secrecy.

Dr. Larson: There seems to be support for this idea—for some kind of impartial and independent and highly qualified body that would pass upon the military budget and would be available to Congressmen and Senators to answer their questions.

Representative Rosenthal: Would you recommend that this group be paid by an outside source, paid by the government, or not paid?

Professor Kistiakowsky: It would certainly have to have paid staff, because it would need full-time professionals. Whether the group itself should be paid or not, I have no strong feelings about. I would say certainly that there has to be sufficient acceptance of such a group by the executive branch so that the group would have access to classified information, because without access to intelligence estimates it is extremely difficult to challenge military planners.

Professor York: One has to be careful to see to it that the Department of Defense doesn't pre-empt this particular idea. It needs to be done either at the White House level or in Congress, or maybe there should be two, one of each.

Senator Saxbe: I seriously question whether any group could perform this mission except a group of Congressmen. I don't think anyone else has the capacity, nor do I think anyone would give an outside body the authority to do what needs to be done.

Professor Schultze: It seems to me there are many places where one can set up review groups, where one can build counterweights to the military—if, and only if, you can get a sufficient willingness on the part of the American people not to buy just anything simply because it is wrapped in the flag. Once their product becomes acceptable and usable and respectable, I list the following kind of possibilities:

First, why shouldn't there be a multiplicity of independently financed research centers dealing with military problems in some of our major universities and institutions? We won't do well with this if we let a single institution do it; multiplicity and plurality are needed. With any other major American problem—housing, poverty, education—there is a multiplicity of views available to Congress and Congressional staffs, if they take the trouble to get it.

I don't think classification is so vital that such institutions will need immediate access to all the secret data. I don't think there is a thing Dr. Stone has said, for instance, that depends on classified knowledge. As a matter of fact, you can even say much more that doesn't.

Second, it seems to me not at all impossible to do the same sort of thing in the military area that was done moderately successfully with respect to full employment and economic policy some twenty-two years ago with a joint committee in Congress that had appropriate staff.

This or some similar Congressional institution could provide the focus for an annual debate on the real issues involved in the military budget, and not just on whether the Air Force ought to have a swing-wing plane or not. With a joint committee or similar institution you can get the classified information, if necessary. It would become possible for the Bureau of the Budget to take a much deeper look at military policy than it has in the past, because it would no longer be heresy to question the Joint Chiefs on military assumptions.

It is difficult for anybody outside of the Pentagon to question those assumptions, unless they have the kind of institutional support I am talking about. So it seems to me that there isn't any single body that one would call upon to do this. One must look to a whole series of mechanisms to try to get in the area of military and foreign policy commitments the same kind of multiplicity and plurality of examination that we get in almost every other area of American life.

Representative Mikva: While I am all for the notion of a task force, and even a plurality of task forces, that will give Congress expert knowledge to cope with these issues, I can picture a "defense review office" being quickly captured, or perverted, by the same forces that now run the Armed Services Committee and the Appropriations Committee.

Representative Wolff: I sat on the House Science and Astronautics Committee. I have "top secret" security clearance. When I tried to get information about what was going on in the manned orbiting laboratory program I was told it was classified. This is the root of the problem: We have to base decisions on fact, and if we can't get the facts we can't make the decisions.

One thing that might perhaps come out of these discussions is reconstitution of this group as an *ad hoc* advisory body to Congress, to make available to Congress the various disciplines that would guide us. We do not have the necessary information available to us now.

Professor Rodberg: In a certain sense Congress suffers from too much information today. It is deluged with technical data and evaluations and doesn't know how to handle them—primarily because it has not developed its own way of considering national needs and priorities.

Congress has been mouse-trapped over the last thirty years by the evolution of the executive branch into a technology-based institution. The committee system that Congress had before the government evolved in this way has persisted, with the result that Congress tends to look inward toward the executive branch and its programs rather than looking outward toward the country and asking what its needs are, and then confronting the executive branch with how well it is meeting those needs.

Dr. Schultze described a whole series of weapons systems coming along. They could have been foreseen earlier, but Congress had no perspective from which to consider whether they should be allowed to proceed to the point where they are today. It seems to me that if Congress is to escape from this kind of bureaucratic trap, it needs new ways of considering the budget. It needs a way of formulating a national budget that isn't divided along agency lines but along the lines of national needs, so that it can ask: What are we doing in education? Or, how well is the country educating the populace for the rapidly changing technological age we live in? Out of such a debate the committees confronted with requests from the various agencies would have guidelines. In this way Congress could get a handle on the military budget and also put the nation's other needs into better perspective.

And I wonder why Congress could not, after sitting passively and receiving the President's State of the Union message, engage in a rather extended debate early in the spring—its own State of the Nation examination—instead of waiting for the "revealed word" from the executive branch.

Representative Mikva: I have been as frustrated as anyone— perhaps more because I am a freshman Representative—by the notion that there are things I am not supposed to know even though I am supposed to vote on them.

I read the House debate on the ABM. The Armed Services Committee Chairman, Mendel Rivers, stood on the floor and said, "If you knew what I know about the Soviet Union you wouldn't be standing up here, Congressman Yates." And then he walked off the floor. I suppose that is about as powerful an argument as he could make. But I don't think there is a political handle to the rollback of secrecy, even though I would like to see an effort made on it.

I think the handle is more like what Congressman Leggett was talking about—doing for the military part of the budget what has been done effectively for the domestic side of the budget. We ought to cut the defense budget by a percentage rather than by specific programs. Equally important, we ought to cut the size of our standing armed forces by a percentage.

We have spent a trillion four hundred billion dollars for defense since World War II, and we are not secure.

Professor Galbraith: I would urge that at least some consideration be given to a panel which lives outside of the classified system and has the freedom that that accords. I spent a good part of my life with one degree or another of access to classified information. I have said many times that I never learned from a classified document anything I couldn't get earlier or later from *The New York Times*.

Once you assume that a body of this sort has to have access to classified information, by that very action you accept the rules and indeed to some extent accept the discipline that is imposed by an apparatus which is, we must face it, part of the present defense against criticism.

Professor Kistiakowsky: Dr. Stone's comments on ABM and MIRV dealt with the past. That is possible to do without classified intelligence information. Military planning is done typically for five years hence. It is exceedingly difficult to learn the reasons why they propose this or that without access to intelligence information. So, although I agree with Dr. Galbraith that this does put one under certain obligations, I think this is the price that may have to be paid.

Professor York: The matter of secrecy will create a problem in any attempt to develop a mechanism for getting political control of this escalating military technology and other escalating factors in the security area.

There needs to be some kind of rollback of secrecy, and this rollback needs to be made in the name of American freedom and American rights. Instead of talking as we always do in the classified world about "need to know," we need a "right to know." In such a rollback we are going to face the same kind of problem we always face in discussing other military issues: if the terms in which you take it up are too small, you are simply going to be snowed with detail and not be able to cope with it. If you start arguing why is A classified, the answer will be, because if we reveal A then B and C may be compromised. If you ask why is B classified, you will be told it is because if we reveal B, A and C may be compromised, and the same applies to C.

You simply have to make a large rollback on the grounds that there is too much secrecy and that it is interfering with the ability to arrive at correct decisions.

I want to second Mr. Goodwin's point that we are arriving at wrong results partly because too many things are classified. Many things are being discussed by too few people. Gross mistakes are being made because plans are not being exposed to persons who ought to review them before they are made final and carried out.

We really must fight—Congress must fight—this tactic of the military establishment to hide behind secrecy, to say "I know a secret" and to reserve the status of credibility to those persons who are "cleared."

Representative Leggett: I would like to see this group of scientists and scholars perpetuated in its educational role. We in the Congress, particularly in the Armed Services Committees, have been isolated from the academic community. We are in a total military environment on the House Armed Services Committee; we don't hear outside witnesses. The scientists and educators and economists can be very helpful to Congress in providing us with information.

But I don't think a band of scientists should organize themselves in Washington with a staff and call themselves an arms limitation group for advice to the Congress or an anti-defense budget group for relation to miscellaneous members of the Congress, because I believe the effectiveness of the scientific community would be watered down by such an organization.

Dr. Raskin: I would dissent from any suggestion that a new organizational structure of any sort at this stage is going to make a difference in the structure of the national security state, whether it has classified information or not. The structures presently exist to make the tough decisions and the sort of investigations needed, and to question the assumptions within this present structure. The adding on of a paratechnical group with or without classified information will not make that much difference.

It seems to me that if people are concerned about classified information, one of the basic tasks to which Congress should address itself is to get rid of classified information altogether.

There are two other important points that Dr. Stone has raised: He tells us we are headed straight for disaster and that the idea of the common defense, as stated in the Constitution, can no longer be applied in the context of the military structure we now have. The Constitutional concept of common defense does not apply in the context of MIRV, ABM, chemical and biological warfare, police power, and the like.

I would suggest that if we are not just interested in putting better and more clever people at the controls of the national security state, we must begin talking about democracy again. That means we must begin figuring out how people in the communities can make decisions about the way they want their money and their lives spent.

I would suggest that members of Congress should think about preparing mock budgets to be sent to their constituents, should explain how the money is spent, should ask the people whether or not they want their money spent as it now is spent, should begin to hold hearings in states and Congressional districts on the budget and how much of it should be spent for defense, and how much for health, education, welfare, and related programs.

Representative Eckhardt: I was impressed by Dr. Raskin's remark that an institutionalized group would probably not advance us. I suggest that it might even tend to retard us. Everything that has been said indicates that we must cross the type of institutionalized barriers that already exist. We already have in Congress an abundance of arbitrary divisions —committees dealing separately with foreign policy, national defense, education and labor, and other areas. What we really need is to go beyond these divisions and bring together groups of informed persons in fields such as those represented here to make Congress act more meaningfully as a whole body appealing directly to constituents, with each member dealing in a much more generalized field than that which ordinarily falls within the jurisdiction of a committee.

Whenever we set up a structured group, we almost necessarily begin to try to find a balance for the scope of that group—we tend to place persons within certain categories for advice and for action. We need to rise above such divisions and act as we are supposed to act, as representatives of people on rather broad philosophic grounds.

Dr. Barnet: I very much agree with that. We are talking about a basic imbalance of bureaucratic power in the government—an imbalance which should not surprise us, because we have bought the kind of bureaucracy we have with our tax money. If we keep funding it at the present level, we will continue to perpetuate that basic imbalance.

The challenge to Congress is to begin to see this imbalance itself as the primary problem, the threshold problem, setting the framework within which we look at specific technical questions.

There are two practical things Congress could do, starting from that basic assumption.

First, members of Congress of both parties who believe, as I do, that this is the number-one problem of our national life, could constitute themselves as a group, get such outside help as they need—and I think that they could get excellent advice from many quarters around the country—and begin to attack specific manifestations of this problem. There is no reason why one member of Congress should have to fight a lonely battle to get information to which, as a member of a relevant committee, he surely is entitled. A number of members of Congress who have had similar experiences could begin to take up these particular issues together.

Such a group, constituting itself as an *ad hoc* watchdog group or whatever they want to call themselves, should not wait to be accepted by Congress and institutionalized—I think that would be a long time—though that should surely be their goal.

Second, the Government Operations Committee or another appropriate committee might begin to propose machinery within the executive branch, within the budgetary process, whereby real cost effectiveness questions, political cost effectiveness questions, could be raised. My impression is that no effective machinery exists today whereby those parts of the government representing the nonmilitary really have a chance to argue it out with the military in the executive branch on basic questions of allocation of resources.

It seems to me that a real National Security Council would include representatives of agencies responsible for other aspects of national security than the accumulation of weapons. This could be done on Congressional initiative.

Mr. Piel: Congress is well-supplied with committees to monitor the on-going business of government. If it were now to add still another committee to monitor military affairs in relation to foreign affairs, that action would cover only a part of the total question that faces us. Furthermore, it might accomplish nothing more than the creation of another vested interest, another prisoner of the executive agencies that Congress is supposed to keep under surveillance.

I would like to invoke here the precedent of the Temporary National Economic Committee. In 1939, at the end of the Depression, that committee conducted a searching study of the structure of the American economy. The resulting ten-foot shelf of studies, hearings, and reports remains our best single source for reconstructing the national economy as it stood in those days.

I suggest that Congress create a Temporary Joint Committee on the National Security State. Find a more semantically palatable title if you like.

The mission of this committee would be to look at the

institutional structure of the military-industrial complex; at the relationship between military policy and the economic interests that have battened on the expansion of our military establishment; and at the social and political as well as economic cost of this enterprise to American society.

This committee could spend two or three fruitful years in this work and give the American people a picture of the nation they live in. As a temporary committee, it would have no vested interest in any branch of the government, no ambitions for the future to compromise its candor, and no assignment but to hold the mirror up to America.

Representative Eckhardt: Though all of these suggestions raise serious questions of implementation, the best is that of creating a joint committee of Congress on armaments and priorities; at least this could restore the dialogue on defense issues that has been so rare in recent years. It could raise questions of the type raised here at a level that will have sufficient status to impress the American people.

Senator Fulbright: I don't believe the creation of new permanent committees is really the solution. We have all kinds of committees and institutions. We just don't make them work.

You complain that the right people aren't in them, and that is true. But the point is not to create another and another. It is to improve those we have. That means changing the personnel. There is nothing wrong with the existing institutions that better men couldn't cure.

Professor Neal: It has been my experience for a long time that Congress would buy anything in the name of defense and anti-Communism. And I am not sure that has yet been changed, or that it will be changed until there is a further reexamination of the fundamentals.

The dangers are great. One can think of scenarios in which the ABM and MIRV would be developed, in which there would be escalation in Vietnam, in which the whole situation might rapidly become worse.

The only way around this, I think, is for the concerned members of Congress not only to keep up but to increase their fire, knowing that there is wide and growing support in the country.

We have to keep talking about the underlying assumptions, but we can't afford to be too broad. One can talk about a garrison state or national security state, and certainly there is a good deal of evidence that such a state exists. On the other hand, it seems to me that in terms of what we have to do, which is to have political impact on Congress, and to have continuing popular impact on the country, we must operate within the framework as it now exists.

But whatever we do, there is an increasing and crying need that it be done articulately and dramatically now, without waiting any longer. The omens are not at all encouraging.

Representative Edwards: The national security state is a subject that is larger than either Vietnam or ABM. It is perhaps the most important subject on the national agenda, because the national security state obviously creates the Vietnams and ABMs, and many other problems too.

We should note that military budgets come not from Congress but from the White House and the Bureau of the Budget; Congress just rubber-stamps the military budgets as they come. I am certain that if a military budget of seventy billion instead of eighty billion dollars came from the White House, it would largely pass that way. The examination that is given a military budget in the military committees is almost entirely one-sided. There is not even an effort to have a devil's advocate on the other side. I examined one series of hearings which ran to three thousand pages of testimony from three hundred witnesses, 298 of whom worked for the Pentagon or within the military services. The other two represented the National Rifle Association.

The only measuring stick we use now is the precept that we can't afford *not* to appropriate money to start any new system because the Soviets might be doing the same thing and they might be successful.

Perhaps the answer is to start having outside experts at military hearings. Perhaps it is the formula suggested by Representative Leggett to give the military a certain number of dollars and let them get along on it as best they can; that is rather attractive to me. Or perhaps we should have a permanent private organization that conducts hearings with distinguished experts and renders a judgment on what the national security budget should be.

Perhaps a formula could be worked out comparing our military budget with that of the Soviet Union. We know approximately what their budget is, and it happens to be about half of ours. How about a formula allowing our military people the Soviet budget plus twenty per cent? I know it may sound silly, but that would make our military budget next year fifty billion dollars, a nice figure to start with.

Professor Morgenthau: Certainly the Vietnam war is extremely unpopular and it has been opposed time and again by experts in foreign policy and in the affairs of Southeast Asia; but the war goes on.

Certainly we are all agreed on the weaknesses of the military establishment; but the military establishment is still in power.

The question then is, "How do you translate expert knowledge and the popular mood into political realities?" An individual citizen—and even a member of Congress—is enormously handicapped in arguing against the military establishment, because that establishment is not only the guardian of the safety of the United States—which, under present conditions, means the existence of the United States—but it also holds a monopoly of confidential information and exerts very great social power. How are you going to pit your personal judgment against this enormous authority of the military establishment?

I think this can be achieved only if Congress develops an equally authoritative instrument. I could well imagine a joint Congressional committee which subjects the posture statement of the Secretary of Defense to the same kind of scrutiny to which the economic life of the nation is put by the Joint Economic Committee.

One ought not to overestimate the popular opposition and the Congressional opposition to the ABM proposals. It is not, in my view, a foregone conclusion that there will be a majority in the Senate against the ABM. Even if there were, this would be, in terms of the over-all distribution of political power, nothing more than a flash in the pan.

So I think we ought to be concerned not with the Vietnam war *per se* or with the ABM *per se*, but with the over-all distribution of political power. We ought to ask ourselves how we can develop an independent source of authoritative judgment which would have real political power against the established authority of the military.

Professor Schultze: Two themes with many variations have been running through this discussion. They are not necessarily contradictory in all respects, but in terms of emphasis perhaps they are.

The first I would call the national security state theme: There exists in America a complex of institutions constituting an aggressive military establishment tied together through self-interest. So many people profit from it—not necessarily in the narrow sense of corporate profits, but in terms of their own existence, their livelihood—that restructuring it in any fundamental sense would be exceedingly difficult. The basic need is to change both the structure and the fundamental attitudes of the American people with respect to this national security state and its complex institutions.

The other theme has been more pragmatic: We need to provide the public, and particularly the Congress, with instrumentalities and means of evaluating a number of specific aspects of military budgets and policies, as well as foreign policy commitments.

This is the choice in emphasis: fundamental reform of the entire society or institutional reform of the decision-making apparatus.

My own view is that while both arguments have something to them, the national security state approach is wrong. I believe, naïvely perhaps, that the real problem with military budgets and military commitments is that the great majority of the American people will buy anything once it is wrapped in the flag and the Joint Chiefs say it is necessary for security.

It is not primarily a matter of self-interest; it is not primarily a problem of a vicious structure it will take a virtual revolution to change. If you look at the lessons of Vietnam and ABM, what do you really find? Where are they really vulnerable, in the eyes of the people? Vietnam and ABM have one thing in common: poor credibility. It is not that the American people are less worried about some kind of Communist threat— or less imperialistic, if you like. Rather, they have learned for the first time that this machine does not work, that it gives promise after promise of results, and it doesn't produce anything. The oracle is not really an oracle. This has been demonstrated in the case of Vietnam. In the case of ABM, it hopefully will never have to be shown, but a whole panoply of distinguished and respectable professionals is on record contending that it won't work.

It seems to me that this is the key need: Whatever fundamental restructuring must be done in the long run, the need now is to show the American people that what comes out of the Pentagon is not oracular. And that is not terribly hard to reveal once you have developed appropriate instruments for evaluating the relationship of foreign policy commitments to military contingencies to military structures to weapons systems.

So, to sharpen the argument, I come down hard on the

side that says institutional change is needed to bring to the American people not some long-term philosophical restructuring of their attitudes toward the world but information and analysis and fundamental choices with respect to these weapons systems and military decisions.

Dr. Raskin: I would like to respond to Dr. Schultze. I think there may not be total conflict if we look at short-run and long-term ways of going about this. My argument is that there has emerged a national security state and that it is likely to get much worse. But political efforts can cover a wide spectrum of activities, immediate and long-range.

The problem, of course, is that we live in the immediate present. And so the question of MIRV, for example, becomes frightening. But I think we have to look for a way of placing these immediate problems in the larger context of a long-term institutional turn-around.

I would suggest some difficulty with what Dr. Schultze puts forward. I remember that some of the participants in this discussion suggested the idea of a disarmament agency. I drafted a bill and came to serve in the White House as the point of contact on that issue. And the Arms Control and Disarmament Agency, which was to sit as the vested interest for disarmament in the government, turned out to be nothing at all. The problem, if you go the organizational route, is to find something which will not turn out to be nothing.

We can't just form another group at the top and say, you know, Professor Kistiakowsky will talk to you, Dr. Schultze will whisper in somebody else's ear, and everything will be all right. I don't think that works out. I don't think that is the way we can structure anything any more.

I would go forward, I think, with Professor Morgenthau's idea that there should be a way of reviewing all the national security institutions on a continuing basis. But beyond that mechanism on a national level, we have to go, it seems to me, to the idea of beginning to hold budget hearings in the districts and in the states—to ask the people, "How do you want your money spent? We are now spending ninety cents of your tax dollar on this war and past wars. How do you want your money spent?"

If we keep within the bureaucratic structure as it is, we will never be able to mount an attack that will make a difference. If the Vietnam war goes on for the next three years, which is likely—one should not be naïve and think it won't—or if the ABM and MIRV issues continue and get worse, we will be faced with a really radical question: how to confront the political power that exists in the country and restrict it in a new way.

Epilogue: Dimensoins of Security

By Senator J. William Fulbright

The ultimate test of any foreign policy is not its short-term tactical success but its effectiveness in defending the basic values of the national society. When a policy becomes incompatible with, or subversive of, those values, it is a bad policy, regardless of its technical or tactical effectiveness. I think we all agree that the central, commanding goal of American foreign policy is the preservation of constitutional government in a free society. My apprehension is that we are subverting that goal by the very means chosen to defend it.

Confronted in the last generation with a series of challenges from dynamic totalitarian powers, we have felt ourselves compelled, gradually and inadvertently, to imitate some of the methods of our adversaries, seeking to fight fire with fire. I do not share the view that American fears of Soviet and Chinese aggressiveness have been uniformly paranoiac, although I think there have been a fair number of instances of that. My point is that the very objective we pursue—the preservation of a free society—proscribes certain kinds of policies to us even though they might be tactically expedient. We cannot, without doing to ourselves the very injury that we seek to secure ourselves against from foreign adversaries, pursue policies which rely primarily on the threat or use of force, because policies of force are inevitably disruptive of democratic values.

During more than ten years out of the last thirty we have

been engaged in large-scale warfare, and for the rest of that period we have been engaged in the cold war and in ever more costly preparations for war. In the wake of our disappointment with the United Nations in the late 1940s, we have taken it upon ourselves to preserve order and stability in much of the world, purporting to do on our own the things that Wilson and Roosevelt hoped to accomplish through world organization but never dreamed of America doing on its own. As I have said, I am not one of those who believe that these vast commitments were taken on out of delusion or the conscious lust for power. The threat, though exaggerated and distorted in some instances, has been real enough in others, but in either case the effect on our internal life has been the same. War and the chronic threat of war have been carrying us, "gently," by our "habits," toward despotism.

There are times, to be sure, when a threat may seem so great and imminent as to warrant the circumvention of democratic procedure. There are times when war is thrust upon you. But there are times when a threat turns out in retrospect to have been less ominous than it seemed; there are times when we have some choice in the matter of war and peace. Psychologists tell us that our perceptions are only partly reflections of the real world; the other part is determined by our own expectations. I think we have perceived more menace in the world around us than is actually there. We have had more choice than we have known. Korea was perhaps forced upon us; Vietnam was not. Pearl Harbor left us with no choice; the incident in the Gulf of Tonkin left us with ample choice. The Cuban missile crisis may have warranted unusual procedures; the Bay of Pigs and the Dominican Republic patently did not.

Because of the kind of country we are, we cannot, barring the most exceptional circumstances, allow foreign policy to take priority over domestic and constitutional requirements. Given a choice between the use of force and less certain but peaceful methods, it is in our interests to take a chance on

the latter. Given a choice between efficient emergency procedures and cumbersome democratic ones, it is in our interests
to gamble on the latter—in full consciousness of the possibility
that our democratic procedure may cost us embarrassment or
worse in our foreign policy.

It is quite beside the point to contend, as some of the advocates of the anti-ballistic missile have contended, that it is safer
to "err on the side of security," because security is involved
on both sides of the argument. One has to do with the security
of *means*, the other with the security of ends. For three
decades we have been erring on the side of the security of
means, and the consequences of that error are only now
coming clearly into view.

Every nation has a double identity: It is both a *power* engaged in foreign relations and a *society* serving the interests
of its citizens. As a power the nation draws upon but does not
replenish its people's economic, political, and moral resources.
The replenishment of wealth—in this broader-than-economic
sense—is a function of domestic life, of the nation as a society.
In the last three decades the United States has been heavily
preoccupied with its role as the world's greatest power, to the
neglect of its societal responsibilities and at incalculable cost
to its national security. The economic cost is reflected in the
disparity of almost ten to one between federal military expenditures since World War II and regular national budgetary
expenditures for education, welfare, health, and housing. The
political cost is reflected in the steady concentration of power
in the hands of the national executive, in a long-term trend
toward authoritarian government. The moral cost is reflected
in the unhappiness of the American people, most particularly
in the angry alienation of our youth.

Speaking first of the economics of our global role: I have
been told many times that, in terms of our gross national
product, we can well afford to do the things that need to be
done at home without reducing our activities abroad. The

answer to that assertion is that we are not in fact rebuilding our cities; we are not overcoming poverty and building schools and houses on anything approaching a scale commensurate with the need; nor are we effectively combating crime, pollution, and urban and suburban ugliness.

Even if the economic resources were there, the psychological resources are not. The war in Vietnam has drained off not only money but political energy and leadership, and public receptiveness to reform. The war has totally altered the atmosphere of a few years ago, when hopes and confidence were high and the American people seemed willing to embark upon an era of social reform. An excellent start was made with the landmark legislation of 1964 and 1965, but Vietnam cut that short, dividing the country and the Congress and inciting dissent and disorder. These in turn have given rise to a middle-class reaction based on the fear of violence and anarchy. The result is an atmosphere uncongenial to reform, urgently needed though it is. Until the war in Vietnam is ended, there can be no prospect of the nation's more sober and generous instincts reasserting themselves, no prospect of a renewal of the nation's strength at its vital domestic source.

With military expenditures providing the livelihood of some ten per cent of our work force; with 22,000 major corporate defense contractors and another 100,000 subcontractors; with defense plants or installations located in 363 of the 435 Congressional districts; with the Department of Defense spending 7.5 billion dollars on research and development in 1969, making it the largest consumer of research output in the nation —millions of Americans whose only interest is in making a decent living have acquired a vested interest in an economy geared to war. These benefits, once obtained, are not easily parted with. Every new weapons system or military installation soon acquires a constituency. This process is aided and abetted by the perspicacity with which Pentagon officials award lucrative contracts and establish new plants and installations in the districts of influential members of Congress. I have not the slightest doubt that, if the anti-ballistic missile is deployed, it will soon acquire its own powerful constituency, and then we will be saddled with it for reasons wholly independent of its ostensible military utility.

According to current intelligence calculations, made in terms of equivalent real purchasing power, the Russians are spending only three-fourths as much as we are on defense. Nonetheless we are told that they threaten to pull ahead of us in strategic weapons and we must be prepared to counter that threat. I do not understand why they should be getting so much more for their money than we are. Perhaps the fault lies in inferior American efficiency—a disconcerting thought. Perhaps it lies in the lack of legislative oversight of the defense budget comparable in rigor and thoroughness to that exercised over the much smaller budgets of the other departments.

By any standard the amounts spent on defense have become staggeringly disproportionate to the rest of the economy. It fills me with dismay when Department of Defense officials suggest that, as part of a "grand design" for strategic policy, we may be forced to "win" an arms race with the Russians by relying on our superior resources to spend them into bankruptcy.

Quite as inevitably as if it were deliberate, our imperial role in the world has generated a trend toward authoritarian government. Vested by the Constitution *exclusively* in the Congress, the power to initiate war has now passed under the virtually exclusive control of the executive. The "dog of war," which Jefferson thought had been tightly leashed to the legislature, has now passed under the virtually exclusive control of the executive. The President's powers as commander in chief, which Hamilton defined as "nothing more than the supreme command and direction of the military and naval forces," are now interpreted as conferring upon the President full constitutional power to commit the armed forces to conflict without the consent of Congress. On the one hand it is asserted that the initiation of an all-out nuclear war could not possibly await Congressional authorization; on the other hand it is contended that limited wars are inappropriate for congressional action. There being, to the best of my knowledge, no other kinds of war besides "limited" and "unlimited," it would seem that the Congressional war power has been effectively nullified.

The treaty power of the Senate has also been effectively usurped. Once regarded as the only constitutional means of making a significant foreign commitment, with executive agreements confined to matters of routine or triviality, the treaty has now been reduced to only one of a number of methods of entering binding foreign engagements. In current usage the term "commitment" is used to refer to engagements deriving sometimes from treaties but more often from executive agreements and even simple, sometimes casual, declarations.

Thailand provides an interesting illustration. Under the SEATO Treaty the United States has only two specific obligations to Thailand: to act "in accordance with its constitutional processes" in the event that Thailand is overtly attacked; and to "consult immediately" with the other SEATO allies should Thailand be threatened by subversion. But the presence of fifty thousand American troops in Thailand, assigned there by the executive acting entirely on its own authority, creates a *de facto* commitment going far beyond the SEATO Treaty. In addition, on March 6, 1962, former Secretary of State Dean Rusk and Thai Foreign Minister Thanat Khoman issued a joint declaration in which Secretary Rusk expressed "the firm intention of the United States to aid Thailand, its ally and historic friend, in resisting Communist aggression and subversion." This obviously goes far beyond the SEATO Treaty.

An even more striking illustration of the upgrading of a limited agreement into a *de facto* military obligation is provided by the series of agreements negotiated for the maintenance of bases in Spain. Initiated under an executive agreement in 1953, the bases agreement was significantly upgraded by a joint declaration issued by Secretary Rusk and Spanish Foreign Minister Castiella in 1963 asserting that a "threat to either country" would be the occasion for each to "take such action as it may consider appropriate within the framework of its constitutional processes." In strict constitutional law, this agreement, whose phrasing closely resembles that of our multilateral security treaties, would be binding on no one except for Mr. Rusk himself; in fact it is what might be called the "functional equivalent" of a treaty ratified by the Senate. Acknowledging even more explicitly the extent of our *de facto* commitment to Spain, General Earle G. Wheeler, the chairman of the Joint Chiefs of Staff, acting under instructions from Secretary Rusk, provided Spanish military authorities in 1968 with a secret memorandum asserting that the presence of American armed forces in Spain constituted a more significant security guarantee than would a written agreement.

Quite aside from questions of the merit or desirability of these commitments, the means by which they were incurred must be a matter of great concern to anyone who is concerned with the integrity of our constitutional processes. For at least thirty years power over our foreign relations has been flowing into the hands of the executive. So far has this process advanced that, in the recently expressed view of the Senate Committee on Foreign Relations, "it is no longer accurate to characterize our government, in matters of foreign relations, as one of separated powers checked and balanced against each other." To a limited extent this constitutional imbalance has come about as the result of executive usurpation; to a greater extent it has been caused by the failure of Congress to meet its responsibilities and defend its prerogatives in the field of foreign relations; but most of all it has been the result of chronic warfare and crisis, which all but inevitably result in the concentration of powers.

Under circumstances of continuing threat to the national

security, it is hardly surprising that the military itself should have become an active, and largely unregulated, participant in the policy-making process. Bringing to bear a degree of discipline, unanimity, and strength of conviction seldom found among civilian officials, the able and energetic men who fill the top ranks of the armed services have acquired an influence on the nation's security policy disproportionate to their numbers. The Department of Defense itself has become a vigorous partisan in our politics, exerting great influence on the President, on the military committees of Congress, on the "think tanks" and universities to which it parcels out lucrative research contracts, and on public opinion. I was disturbed to learn that the Department of the Army actually planned a national publicity campaign, involving exhibits and planted magazine articles to be solicited from civilian scientists, in order to "sell" the ABM to the American public and to counteract the criticisms of Congressmen and the scientific community.

Let me emphasize that the danger I perceive here is not military men but *militarism*. Applying the same principle to the executive as a whole, the danger of executive dominance over our foreign relations has nothing to do with the wisdom or lack of it of individual officials. A threat to democracy arises from *any* great concentration of unregulated power. I would no more want unregulated power to be wielded by the Congress than by the executive or the military—or the Senate Committee on Foreign Relations. The principle is an old and familiar one, and is just as valid today as it was when Jefferson expressed it in the simple maxim, "Whatever power in any government is independent, is absolute also."

Congress has recently shown a growing awareness of the need for restoring a degree of constitutional balance in the making of our foreign policy. To a great extent this new attitude has been reflected in the debate on the anti-ballistic missile and a general disposition to bring the military budget under the same scrutiny that has always been applied to the budgets of the civilian agencies. These, I believe, are hopeful and necessary steps, but in the long run it is unlikely that constitutional government can be preserved solely by the vigorous exercise of legislative authority. No matter what safeguards of attitude and procedure we employ, a foreign policy of chronic warfare and intervention has its own irreversible dynamic, and that is toward authoritarian government.

The success of a foreign policy, as we have been discovering, depends not only on the availability of military and economic resources but, at least as much, upon the support given it by our people. As we have also been discovering, that support cannot be gained solely by eloquent entreaty, much less by the devices of public relations. In the long run it can only be secured by devising policies which are broadly consistent with the national character and traditional values of the society, and these—products of the total national experience—are beyond the reach of even the most effective modern techniques of political manipulation.

History did not prepare the American people for the kind of role we are now playing. From the time of the framing of the Constitution to the two world wars our experience and values—if not our uniform practice—conditioned us not for the unilateral exercise of power but for the placing of limits upon it. Perhaps it was a vanity, but we supposed that we could be an example for the world—an example of rationality and restraint. We supposed, as Woodrow Wilson put it, that a rational world order could be created embodying "not a balance of power but a community of power; not organized rivalries, but an organized common peace."

Our practice has not lived up to that ideal, but from the earliest days of the Republic the ideal has retained its hold upon us, and every time we have acted inconsistently with it—not just in Vietnam but every time—a hue and cry of opposition has arisen. When the United States invaded Mexico, two former Presidents and one future President—John Quincy Adams, Martin Van Buren, and Abraham Lincoln—denounced the war as violating American principles. The senior of them, John Quincy Adams, is said even to have expressed the hope that General Taylor's officers would resign and his men desert. When the United States fought a war with Spain and then suppressed the patriotic resistance to American rule of the Philippines, the ranks of opposition were swelled with two former Presidents, Benjamin Harrison and Grover Cleveland, with Senators and Congressmen including the Speaker of the House of Representatives, and with such distinguished individuals as Andrew Carnegie and Samuel Gompers.

The dilemma of contemporary American foreign policy is that, while becoming the most powerful nation ever to have existed on the earth, the American people have also carried forward their historical mistrust of power and their commitment to the imposition of restraints upon it. That dilemma came to literal and symbolic fulfillment in 1945 when two powerful new forces came into the world. One was the bomb at Hiroshima, representing a quantum leap to a new dimension of undisciplined power. The other was the United Nations Charter, representing the most significant effort ever made toward the restraint and control of national power. Both were American inventions, one the product of our laboratories, the other the product of our national experience. Incongruous though they are, these are America's legacies to the modern world: the one manifested in Vietnam and the nuclear arms race, the other in the hope that these may yet be brought under control.

The incongruity between our old values and our new unilateral power has greatly troubled the American people. It has much to do, I suspect, with the current student rebellion. Like a human body reacting against a transplanted organ, our body politic is reacting against the alien values which, in the name of security, have been grafted upon it. We cannot—and dare not—divest ourselves of power, but we have a choice as to how we will use it. We can try to ride out the current convulsion in our society and adapt ourselves to a new role as the world's nuclear vigilante. Or we can try to adapt our power to our traditional values, never allowing it to become more than a means toward domestic societal ends, while seeking every opportunity to discipline it within an international community.

We cannot resolve this dilemma by choosing to "err on the side of security," because security is the argument for both sides. The real question is: which represents the more promising approach to security in its broader dimension? A democracy simply cannot allow foreign policy to become an end in itself, or anything more than an instrument toward the central dominating goal of securing democratic values within our own society. I would indeed lay it down as a fairly confident prediction that, if American democracy is destroyed within the next generation, it will not be destroyed by the Russians or the Chinese but by ourselves, by the very means we use to defend it. That is why it seems to me so urgent for us to change the emphasis of our policy, from the security of means to the security of ends.

The Contributors

RICHARD BARNET is Co-director of the Institute for Policy Studies in Washington, D.C. Formerly a consultant to the Department of Defense and a staff member of the United States Arms Control and Disarmament Agency, he is the author of *Intervention and Revolution*.

KENNETH E. BOULDING is Chairman of the Department of Economics at the University of Colorado in Boulder. He is a member of the Institute for Peace Research and is a past President of the American Economic Association. He is the author of many articles, reviews, and books, among them *Economic Analysis, Reconstruction of Economics,* and *The Meaning of the Twentieth Century*.

GEORGE BROWN, JR., was elected to the United States House of Representatives in 1962. He is from Los Angeles County, California, and was employed by the city of Los Angeles for twelve years in engineering and management. He is a member of the House Science and Astronautics Committee and of the Foreign Policy Steering Committee of the Democratic Study Group.

PHILLIP BURTON has represented the city of San Francisco in the United States House of Representatives since 1965. Elected to the California State Assembly in 1956, he was the youngest member and the only Democrat to defeat an incumbent Republican that year in California. He is a member of the Committee on Education and Labor.

JOHN CONYERS, JR., was elected to the United States House of Representatives in 1964. He is a Democrat from Detroit, Michigan. He has been active in civil rights, labor, and police-community activities and has written widely on the role of blacks in American politics. He is a member of the House Committee on Judiciary.

ROBERT C. ECKHARDT is a Democrat from Harris County, Texas. He was a practicing attorney until he entered Congress in 1967. He served in the Texas House of Representatives from 1958 to 1966. A licensed pilot who has taught flying, he is a member of the Subcommittee on Space Sciences and Applications.

DON EDWARDS was elected to the United States House of Representatives in 1962. He is a Democrat from San Jose, California. A former naval intelligence officer and FBI agent, he is a past president of Americans for Democratic Action and has been active in civil liberties activities. He is a member of the Committee on Judiciary.

RICHARD A. FALK is a Professor of International Law at the Center for Advanced Study in the Behavioral Sciences at Stanford University, California. The author of *The Strategy of World Order* and *Legal Order in a Violent World*, he has served as Counsel to the Senate Foreign Relations Committee. He has also served as Counsel before the International Court of Justice, and on the United States Arms Control and Disarmament Agency.

BRIGADIER GENERAL WILLIAM WALLACE FORD retired from the United States Army after combat service in Europe during World War II and postwar service in Panama, France, and

Germany. He now teaches mathematics at the University of Massachusetts in Amherst.

DONALD M. FRASER has been a member of the United States House of Representatives since 1963. He is a Democrat from Minneapolis, Minnesota, and was a State senator from 1954 to 1962. He is a member of the House Committee on Foreign Affairs and is Chairman of the Democratic Study Group, the liberal caucus of House Democrats.

J. WILLIAM FULBRIGHT has served in the United States Congress since 1943. A member of the House of Representatives from 1943 to 1944, he was elected to the Senate in 1944. A Democrat from Arkansas, he is the author of the Fulbright program for the international exchange of scholars. He is Chairman of the Committee on Foreign Relations and is a member of the Senate Finance Committee. He is the author of *The Arrogance of Power* and *Old Myths: New Realities*.

JOHN KENNETH GALBRAITH, author of *The Great Crash, The Affluent Society, The Liberal Hour,* and *The New Industrial State,* is Professor of Economics at Harvard University, Cambridge, Mass. He was a member of the Board of Editors of *Fortune* magazine from 1943 to 1948 and Ambassador to India from 1961 to 1963.

RICHARD N. GOODWIN was a Special Assistant to President Kennedy and President Johnson. He served as Deputy Assistant Secretary of State for Inter-American Affairs from 1961 to 1963 and is the author of *Triumph or Tragedy: Reflections on Vietnam*.

GEORGE McT. KAHIN is Professor of Government and Director of the Southern Asia Program at Cornell University, Ithaca, N.Y. He is the author of *Nationalism and Revolution in Indonesia* and *Major Governments in Asia,* and co-author (with John Lewis) of *The United States in Vietnam*.

ROBERT W. KASTENMEIER has been a member of the House of Representatives since 1959. He is a Democrat from Madison, Wisconsin. Formerly a practicing attorney, he is a member of the House Judiciary Committee. In 1965 he conducted local hearings on American Vietnam policy and published *Hearings on Vietnam: Voices from the Grassroots.*

GEORGE B. KISTIAKOWSKY is a Professor of Chemistry at Harvard University, Cambridge, Mass. He served as a member of the President's Science Advisory Committee from 1957 to 1963 and as Special Assistant to the President for Science and Technology from 1959 to 1961.

ARTHUR LARSON, author of *A Republican Looks at His Party* and *Preventing World War III: Some Proposals,* and co-author (with Don R. Larson) of *Vietnam and Beyond,* is Director of the World Rule of Law Research Center at Duke University, Durham, N.C. He served as Under-Secretary of Labor from 1954 to 1956, Director of the United States Information Agency from 1956 to 1957, and Special Assistant to the President from 1957 to 1958. He was also Special Consultant to the State Department from 1958 to 1961.

ROBERT L. LEGGETT has been a member of the United States House of Representatives since 1963. A Democrat from Vallejo, California, he is a member of the House Armed Services Committee and is the ranking member of the Anti-Submarine Warfare Committee.

RICHARD D. MCCARTHY is a Democrat from Buffalo, New York. A member of the House of Representatives since 1965, he is a former newspaperman and public-relations executive. A member of the Committee on Public Works, he has been instrumental in investigating Defense Department activities in the fields of chemical and biological warfare.

GEORGE S. MCGOVERN is a Democratic Senator from South

Dakota. He holds a Ph.D. in History and is a former Professor of History and Government at Dakota Wesleyan University, Mitchell, S.D. After serving in the United States House of Representatives from 1957 to 1961, he was named Food for Peace Director and Special Assistant to President Kennedy in 1961. He is Chairman of the Senate Committee on Nutrition and Human Needs and was a candidate for the Democratic presidential nomination in the summer of 1968.

ABNER J. MIKVA is a Democrat from Chicago, Illinois. Elected to the United States House of Representatives in 1968, he has been a practicing attorney since 1952. He was a member of the Illinois State Legislature for ten years and was Chairman of the Illinois House Judiciary Committee. He is a member of the House Committee on Judiciary.

HANS J. MORGENTHAU is Professor of Political Science and Modern History and Director of the Center for Study of American Foreign Policy at the University of Chicago. The author of *Politics Among Nations, The Purpose of American Politics, Politics in the Twentieth Century,* and *A New Foreign Policy for the United States,* he has also served as a consultant to the Department of Defense.

FRED WARNER NEAL is Professor of International Relations and Government at Claremont Graduate School, Claremont, California, and is a consultant to the Center for the Study of Democratic Institutions. The author of *Yugoslavia and the New Communism* and *War and Peace and Germany,* he was former Washington correspondent for the *Wall Street Journal* and a consultant in Russian Affairs to Chief of Foreign Research, State Department.

GAYLORD A. NELSON is a Democratic Senator from Wisconsin. Until his election to the United States Senate in 1962, he had been Governor of Wisconsin for two terms. He is Chairman of the Senate Employment and Manpower Subcommittee and is the only man remaining in the Senate to have voted against the 1965 appropriations for the Vietnam war.

GERARD PIEL has been Editor and Publisher of *Scientific American* since 1948. The author of *Science in the Cause of Man*, he was Science Editor of *Life* magazine from 1939 to 1945.

MARCUS RASKIN is Co-director of the Institute for Policy Studies, Washington, D.C. He served as Legislative Counsel to twelve Democratic Congressmen from 1958 to 1961 and was Staff Editor of the *Liberal Papers*, published in 1961. A member of the National Security Council staff from 1961 to 1962, he served as Education Advisor in the Office of the President and was a member of the United States Disarmament Delegation in Geneva. He is the co-author (with Bernard Fall) of *Vietnam Reader* and author of *Being and Doing*.

GEORGE W. RATHJENS is Professor of Political Science at Massachusetts Institute of Technology, Cambridge. Author of *The Future of the Strategic Arms Race: Options for the 1970's*, he was Chief Scientist, Advanced Research Projects Agency, Department of Defense, in 1961. From 1962 to 1964 he was Deputy Assistant Director, United States Arms Control and Disarmament Agency; and from 1965 to 1968 he was the Director of the Weapons Systems Evaluation Division, Institute for Defense Analysis.

LEONARD RODBERG is Associate Professor and Associate Chairman of the Department of Physics at the University of Maryland, College Park. From 1961 to 1966 he was Chief of Policy Research in the Science and Technology Bureau of the United States Arms Control and Disarmament Agency.

BENJAMIN S. ROSENTHAL is a Democrat from Queens, New York, and has been a member of the United States House of Representatives since 1962. A practicing attorney before entering Congress, he is a member of the Foreign Affairs Committee and Government Operations Committee. He is Chairman of the Special Inquiry on Consumer Representation in the Federal Government and is the principal sponsor of legislation to create a Department of Consumer Affairs.

WILLIAM FITTS RYAN has been a member of the House of Representatives since 1962. He is a Democrat from New York City and is one of the founders of the New York Democratic Reform Movement. An assistant district attorney for New York from 1950 to 1957, he was the Reform Democratic candidate for Mayor of New York City in 1965. He is a member of the Committee on Interior and Insular Affairs and the Committee on Science and Astronautics.

WILLIAM B. SAXBE is a Republican Senator from Ohio. Before his election to the United States Senate in 1968, he was majority Leader and Speaker of the Ohio House of Representatives and was Attorney General of Ohio for eight years. He is a member of the Committee on Labor and Public Welfare, the Committee on Aeronautical and Space Sciences, and the Special Committee on Aging.

CHARLES L. SCHULTZE is a Professor of Economics at the University of Maryland, College Park, and is a Senior Fellow at Brookings Institution. He was the Director of the Bureau of the Budget from 1965 to 1968 and was a member of the staff of the Council of Economic Advisers from 1952 to 1958. He is the author of *National Income Analysis*.

JEREMY J. STONE, a member of the Executive Council of the Federation of American Scientists, is now working in Washington, D.C., as an International Affairs Fellow of the Council on Foreign Relations. He is the author of two books, *Containing the Arms Race* and *Strategic Persuasion: Arms Limitation through Dialogue*. He was formerly with the

Hudson Institute and was a Research Associate at the Harvard Center for International Affairs from 1964 to 1966.

ADAM WALINSKY served as Legislative Aide to the late Senator Robert F. Kennedy.

LESTER L. WOLFF is a Democrat representing Nassau County, New York. Before his election to the United States House of Representatives in 1964, he was Chairman of the Board of the Coordinated Marketing Agency from 1945 to 1964 and was a television moderator. He is a member of the Committee on Science and Astronautics.

HERBERT F. YORK is Professor of Physics at the University of California at San Diego, where he served as Chancellor from 1961 to 1964. From 1958 to 1961 he was Director, Defense Research and Engineering, Department of Defense. He was Vice-Chairman of the President's Science Advisory Committee from 1965 to 1966.